What Others Are Saying About This Book

"The main reason that start-ups fail is that the entrepreneur's effort and energy go into growing the business, with none left for growing themselves. That's where a mentor comes in. This easily-accessible book provides a recipe for finding and using a mentor to best effect."

—**David Clutterbuck**, international mentoring, coaching, leadership expert, Special Ambassador/Co-founder of European Mentoring & Coaching Council (UK).

"Dr. McGowan provides a welcome guiding light to those who have an important message to share with the world. You don't have to choose between earning a living and doing what you were born to do—you can do both!—while not having to manage a company to make it happen.

This book illustrates each step in your path from identifying your purpose and vision to creating a success plan, and it reveals the secret of all success as a solopreneur: finding the right mentor and creating the right you to be mentored. Follow the doctor's advice to use the proven power of mentors to make money while pursuing your passion."

—**Matt Champagne PhD**, researcher, serial entrepreneur, author, & survey sensei (USA).

"A complete, comprehensive, and easy-to-digest guide for any solopreneur who sees the benefits of working with a mentor."

—**Nancy Leinweber**, freelance writer (Adelaide, South Australia).

"This is a 'must have, must-read' book for anyone thinking of becoming a solopreneur or who is already a solopreneur. When I think back to the beginning of my journey, I was not provided a resource as valuable as this to prepare me for the roller-coaster ride that lay ahead. The author recognizes the need for personal and professional mentoring. All too often, mentor programs focus on the professional growth of the mentee and fail to look at the personal side of the equation. This book clearly demonstrates the importance and significance of doing so. The author also recognizes that both the mentor and solopreneur will learn and grow together. This has become a differentiating factor when deciding on whether mentoring is the choice for each person.

As a solopreneur wanting to continue your journey, this is the book that you must have. Can you afford not to?"

—Doug Lawrence, President, TalentC® - People Services Inc. (Canada).

"This book hits squarely at the heart of mentoring and its critical importance. As a guide to developing an effective, healthy mentoring relationship, Virginia's book is an exceptional 'how to' manual for the much-neglected solopreneur. Practical, accessible, and containing clear advice, it's a must-read for anyone in business by themselves."

—Dan Pontefract, best-selling author of Open to Think, The Purpose Effect, and Flat Army (Canada).

"Being a solopreneur is a scary and lonely endeavor with many sleepless nights worrying about decisions and visions. As Virginia so very clearly states, 'You don't have to do it alone!' This book takes the fear out of being a solopreneur by providing a roadmap for what to do to have your questions answered and your future clarified by someone who's 'been there and done that.' No matter your level of experience, it will provide answers for you to take the fear out of doing business and replace it with the fun you always wanted it to be."

—S. Paul Kearley, President, IBC Impact Business Communication, Inc. (Canada).

"This is a very clearly written book on an important and growing issue in business. As job markets change and global unemployment increases, more and more people are turning to self-employment by becoming solopreneurs and mentoring becomes a vital source of support for these people. Ginny says it how it is with her direct style of writing. The honesty is refreshing and the clear sense of 'practical wisdom' contained within these pages is inspiring. The vignettes are insightful, practical and grounded in a lived reality. This is a 'must-read' for anyone looking to work with the right mentor to sustain their business."

—Bob Garvey PhD, mentoring researcher, author, co-founder of the European Mentoring & Coaching Council, and multiple award recipient for leadership in mentoring (UK).

"What an amazing little book! Of high value to the mentee and the mentor. Step-by-step, you are shown how to develop the perfect mentoring relationship, and if that relationship gets rocky, you are given the skills to save it. You could use these clear steps to organize your life."

—**Philip Whittaker**, solopreneur (retired) (Canada).

"A much-needed book to fill the void in the business mentoring field for niche solopreneurs. This book is written in an engaging, energizing and pragmatic way to make a busy solopreneur sit up and find themselves a mentor! The unique intertwining of personal and business planning support is handled beautifully. Virginia is also not afraid to tackle the tricky topics of evaluation and how to say goodbye, both more difficult topics outside of an organizational program. I recommend this practical and very readable guide to any solopreneur who wants to tap into the powerful support of a mentor."

—**Lis Merrick**, Managing Director, Coach Mentoring Ltd. (UK)

Harness the Power of Mentoring

How to Find and Work With the Right Mentor

A Guide for the Solopreneur

Virginia McGowan PhD

1st Edition

BUSINESS MENTORING
SOLUTION

Charlottetown PE Canada

Harness the Power of Mentoring: How to Find and Work With the Right Mentor—A Guide for the Solopreneur.
Published by
The Business Mentoring Solution
An Imprint of McGowan & Co.: The Write Edit Group
255 Richmond Street
Charlottetown PE C1A 1J7 Canada
https://businessmentoringsolution.com

10 9 8 7 6 5 4 3 2 1

A copy of this book is retained by Library and Archives Canada.

Copyright © 2018 by The Business Mentoring Solution. All Rights Reserved. No part of this work, including the exterior and interior design and icons, may be reproduced or transmitted in any form, by any means (electronic, photocopying, recording, or otherwise) without the prior written permission of the publisher except for the inclusion of brief quotations in a review.

ISBN Print edition 978-1-7750287-3-4
ISBN PDF eBook edition: 978-1-7750287-4-1

Printed in the United States of America.

McGowan & Co.: The Write Edit Group
Tel: +1-902-566-5462
Executive Director: Richard Forsyth MA
Senior Writer, Researcher, Editor: Virginia McGowan PhD
www.writeeditgroup.com

Contents

Foreword	v
Dedication	vii
About the Author	viii
Disclaimer	xii
1. Solopreneurs and Business Mentors: *Why you should consider a mentor*	1
2. Values, Purpose, Vision, and Goals: *What do you want to achieve?*	19
3. Doing an Inventory: *Discover what you need NOW*	29
4. The Right Mentor for You: *Finding the best fit for a solopreneur*	41
5. Working with Your Mentor: *How to develop and nurture a healthy mentoring relationship*	51
6: Fail to Plan, Plan to Fail: *Create a strategy for solopreneur success*	61
7: Taking and Giving Feedback: *Even when it's hard to hear or say*	77
8. Evaluate Your Progress: *Learn from mistakes, celebrate successes*	89
9. How to Say Thanks and Goodbye: *When your mentorship has run its course*	97
10. Next Steps: *Am I ready to be a mentor to a solopreneur?*	111
Afterword	120
Appendix: *Resources to Support Your Mentorship*	122
Products and Services	140
Join Me Online	142
For Orders and Inquiries	143
Index	145
Endnotes	147

Supporting Solopreneur Success

Foreword

Business mentoring was once defined as a relationship between a powerful mentor and a subordinate, often naïve, protégé. The mentor would assist by paving the way for the protégé to the inner circle of an organization. Not so anymore.

Today's mentoring relationship is all about personal and professional development. It's about slowing down and really thinking about what we want and need to do. It's about deepening the mentee's ability to think critically, openly, and to make decisions.

The mentor's role has changed accordingly to one who listens, probes, encourages, challenges, and inspires. This is the message of Virginia's book *Harness the Power of Mentoring: How to Find and Work with the Right Mentor—A Guide for the Solopreneur*. It's a theme I whole-heartedly endorse.

With her background in anthropology, and a holistic and humanistic perspective on the human condition, Virginia is the best person to author this book. She has heard the stories of solopreneurs and the positive effect of having the right mentor. With her strong background in mentoring, program design, and her real work within the mentor-mentee relationship, Virginia has the street creds to deliver this message. She delivers it in a way that makes sense allowing the reader to easily absorb and embrace the message.

I became aware of Virginia's passion for mentoring while I was a mentor in the Prince Edward Island Business Women's Association (PEIBWA) project Business Mentoring for Women Entrepreneurs. I witnessed firsthand her deep understanding of the mentoring relationship, her engagement with mentors and mentees, and her ability to mentor the participants in a very practical approach to creating mutually beneficial partnerships.

With more than 30 years' experience operating businesses, I focus on business development and customer relations for my company, Navigate Food Safety Solutions. My role is to understand the challenges facing our clients and help them find the very best solutions based on their business imperatives and company needs. We create a step-by-step roadmap; our team walks with customers every step of the way to train, coach, and mentor them through to achieving their goals. They learn to make better decisions by strengthening their own understanding of their exact needs.

It's paramount for us as business owners to recognize that our thinking is only as good as our ability to challenge and question continuously. Better thinking depends on how open we are to new ideas, how evidence based our decision-making is, and how capable we are of getting things done.

We often ask ourselves "Does this make sense?" We must also learn to ask the tougher, deeper question: "What about this doesn't make sense?"

For a solopreneur, finding the right mentor can be a game changer. The right mentor will guide you to open up, to examine evidence before you act, and apply that brand of thinking to reach your true potential. You'll avoid the pitfall of jumping into action without thinking the situation through and becoming overwhelmed, or underwhelmed, by the results. The challenge for solopreneurs who are in business on their own: they are most often without larger support networks.

The solution is to understand and seek the right mentor for you and your business.

I agreed to write this foreword because I believe that the fastest growing segment of entrepreneurs—solopreneurs— need to hear, learn, and apply this message. Mentoring can transform business culture. It's time that solopreneurs join the transformation.

Going solo does not mean you have to go it alone.

—Maureen Campbell Hanley

Navigate Food Safety Solutions Inc.

www.navigatefoodsafety.com

Dedication

This book is dedicated to those valiant souls, the solopreneurs, who take risks, live their passions, and contribute so much, with my thanks for sharing their stories.

Go ahead! Change your world.

About the Author

Virginia McGowan PhD

I believe that with the right mentor, anything is possible.

I had amazing mentors during my early years, people who helped me develop as a person and a professional. In turn, I've spent my profesional life mentoring others: students, colleagues, or friends in need.

As I began a new career as an entrepreneur, it made sense that I looked for mentors to help me carve a new path. Then it was time to pay it forward.

As an applied social scientist (MA and PhD in anthropology), I'm passionate about helping others overcome adversity, reach their potential, and realize their aspirations and dreams. And, I know of what I speak when I address solopreneurs: I'm the sole proprietor of The Business Mentoring Solution (https://businessmentoringsolution.com), an imprint of my research, writing, and editing consultancy McGowan & Co.: The Write Edit Group (www.writeeditgroup.com).

I became deeply interested in the potential for mentoring for personal and professional development when I realized just how significant my own mentoring experience had been for me. I joined the Cherie Blair Foundation for Women's Business Mentoring Programme in 2015. Following completion of mentor training, I was matched with mentees from Kenya, the Caribbean, and Indonesia.

I'm also a mentor with the Canadian business women's organization Forum for Women Entrepreneurs. I was certified in 2016 as a mentoring program manager.

I recently had the opportunity to research, design, and pilot a business mentoring program for women entrepreneurs under contract to the Prince Edward Island Business Women's Association (PEIBWA). It's one of the first structured community-based and evidence-based business mentoring programs in existence in Canada. The program and project are described in a book published in November 2017 by the University of Prince Edward Island's Island Studies Press.[1]

Need help? I guide solopreneurs to find and work with the right mentor to build a healthy, effective mentoring relationship so they can rise to new heights and realize their true potential. I'm available as a consultant on mentoring program design and evaluation, as a trainer and speaker, and as a professional writer and editor. For enquiries about mentoring, the best way to reach me is: author@thebusinessmentoringsolution.com.

Connect with me! Sign up on my website for a free monthly newsletter. Tell me what you think of this book. Check out my LinkedIn profile, Twitter feed, and Facebook page. The links are in the back sections of this book.

Yours in mentoring,

Ginny

The Business Mentoring Solution

https://www.linkedin.com/in/virginiamcgowanphd/
https://businessmentoringsolution.com

Acknowledgements

While researching this book, I accessed many website postings, reports, and scholarly papers on mentoring. I've not attempted to cite all the authorities and sources consulted in preparation of this book, however, as that would make it unreadable. It would also clutter up this space and make the book much longer than necessary.

Accordingly, I've added a list of helpful resources as an Appendix.

My thinking about business mentoring was influenced by my training and experience with the mentoring program of the Cherie Blair Foundation for Women; the writings of Professors David Clutterbuck. David Megginson, and Bob Garvey; Lois J. Zachary, David A. Stoddard, and Ann Rolfe; and the mentors and mentees in the Prince Edward Island Business Women's Association's (PEIBWA) mentoring program for women entrepreneurs that I developed and piloted. I am particularly thankful to PEIBWA for the opportunity to work on this extraordinary project.

So many others to thank. I am grateful to Nancy Leinweber (Amaroo) for copyediting; Colleen McKie for proofreading (Savvy Fox Author Services); Laurie Forsyth for indexing; Wilco van Eikeren (Recon Design) for cover and logo design and advice on layout; Jill at Revolution Media for formatting in InDesign; Katie at Revolution Media for creating my website; indie author Patti Larsen (Patti Larsen Inc.) for mentorship in self-publishing; Maureen Campbell Hanley (Navigate Food Safety Solutions) for writing the foreword and providing much-needed marketing advice; John Sewuster for advice on promotion; insightful discussions with Doug Lawrence (Talent C®); and the solopreneurs and mentors who agreed to share their stories and experience.

I am particularly indebted to the advance review copy reviewers who contributed so much to improvement of the manuscript. Thank you for your advice and encouragement.

I also appreciate the helping hands and encouragement of family, friends, and colleagues. Richard Forsyth, my patient husband, never lost faith in me and my crazy ideas. My sister Nancy Leinweber cheered me on and spent a sizable chunk of her holiday in Canada copyediting the text.

I also appreciate that my mischievous Havanese, Pepper, restrained from eating the piles of drafts, despite her love of chewing paper, while she kept my toes warm in my office.

The support of John Eggen and my coaches/mentors Christy Tryhus and Adam Dudley from Mission Publishing (a division of Mission Marketing Mentors, Inc.) was critical for keeping me on track during the writing and review stages, publication, and promotion of this book. They provided guidelines, encouragement, and sound advice on layout of text and covers, marketing, and promotion. They made the path forward clearly visible and attainable.

Any errors, omissions, or shortcomings remain my own responsibility.

Disclaimer

This book is intended for educational purposes only to provide information about the subject matter: business mentoring for solopreneurs. The publisher and author make no representations or warranties with respect to the accuracy or completeness of the contents of this work and specifically disclaim all warranties including, without limitation, warranties of fitness for a particular purpose.

No warranty may be created or extended by sales or promotional materials. The advice and strategies contained herein may not be suitable for every situation.

This work is sold with the understanding that the publisher is not engaged in rendering legal, accounting, or other professional services. If professional assistance is required, the services of a competent professional person should be sought. Neither the publisher nor the author shall be liable for damages arising herefrom.

Business mentoring is not a guarantee of entrepreneurial success; although every effort has been made to be as complete and accurate as possible in presenting this information, it is intended as a general guide and not the ultimate source on business mentoring.

The fact that an organization or website is referred to in this work as a citation and/or a potential source of further information does not mean that the author or the publisher endorses the information that the organization or website may provide or recommendations it may make. Further, readers should be aware that internet websites listed in this work may have changed or disappeared between when this work was written and when it is read.

If you do not wish to be bound by the above, you may return this book to the publisher for a full refund.

1

Solopreneurs and Business Mentors

Why you should consider a mentor

> One of the great values of mentors is the ability to see ahead what others cannot see and to help them navigate a course to their destination.
>
> **—John C. Maxwell**, bestselling leadership author.

Every entrepreneur wants to succeed in their business.

Unfortunately, although most people have the drive and passion, few have the full set of skills and experience required for running a business. That's the main reason only half of all small business startups fail in their first five years of operation.[2]

On the other hand, did you know that 70 percent of small businesses survive their first five years of operation when the proprietor has a mentor?[3]

This tells us that small business owners need help from someone who has 'been there, done that,' successfully. Someone who can help them plan their entrepreneurial journey.

And no one needs that help more than the solopreneur. As someone who is in business on their own, they often feel quite isolated, overwhelmed, and frustrated. They don't know where to turn for help. They may not have had firsthand experience in running a business, or even seen how an entrepreneur manages day-to-day or over the long term.

They may feel embarrassed, thinking, "I should know how to do this—everyone else does!"

This book will provide you with what you need to know to find the right mentor for your business and your personality, someone with whom you will 'click' as a solopreneur and who understands that the role of a mentor is to guide, not to coach or direct.

That's not all. You will also learn how to:

- Approach the right person to ask them to be your mentor.

- Develop a healthy and productive mentoring relationship.

- Take and give feedback, even if it's something that's hard to hear or say.

- Get what you need to get out of a mentoring relationship and what to put back in.

- Evaluate your progress and success in reaching your goals.

- Learn when to say 'thanks' and 'goodbye' when the mentoring relationship has run its course.

You may come across some terms in this book that are unfamiliar: mentoring, coaching, mentor, mentee, entrepreneur, solopreneur, and intrapreneur. Don't panic! A list of these terms and how they are used in this book is included at the end of this chapter.

THE SPECIAL CASE OF THE SOLOPRENEUR

Bookstores—real and online—are filled with books, manuals, guidelines, and other resources on mentoring, yet few if any are applicable to the uniqueness of the solopreneur. Most of these sources speak to the important topic of mentoring youth at risk.

Those resources that appear in the business section are geared toward workplace-based mentoring programs. Generally, the programs are run by larger enterprises for their in-house staff as part of the orientation for new hires or the career development process: an experienced and successful career employee takes a (usually, but not always) younger and newer employee under their wing.

The problem is that these situations don't speak to the experiences, mindset, and business practices of your average solopreneur.

What makes a solopreneur so unique? Well…they are flying solo! Many times, at least at the beginning, they are the owner, staff, bookkeeper, marketer, and janitor. They are crazily busy, so when do they have time to network and find others who can help them?

It's more than that, however. Studies—confirmed by my experience working with solopreneurs—show clearly that solopreneurs differ from other entrepreneurs in both business practices and in their mindset. As Marcia Layton-Turner noted in the online magazine *Business 2 Community*, "Solopreneurs are a specific type of entrepreneur who *prefer* to work alone."[4]

The difference between a solopreneur and a conventional entrepreneur may be subtle to discern. Some entrepreneurs work alone *until* they can expand by hiring employees. However, the true solopreneur is more worker than manager. They don't see themselves as delegating work to others, unless it means contracting out specific tasks such as to an accountant or digital marketer.

In fact, although they must rely on others for some tasks, solopreneurs don't intend to add anyone to the business, preferring to make decisions and do the work themselves. Their long-term plan is not to eventually attract a venture capitalist and sell their business, but to fit a certain lifestyle, pursue a personal passion, and have flexibility and control.

The solopreneur has a different approach to branding, tending to focus more on getting the work done and less on marketing than does the entrepreneur.

Conventional entrepreneurs, on the other hand, tend to focus on start-up businesses, preferring to be out connecting and networking while employees produce and deliver the goods and services on which the business depends.[5] They also are more likely to want to sell and move on to start a new business, hence the label "serial entrepreneur."

> The solopreneur has a unique set of aspirations, objectives, and attitude towards being in business.

Most solopreneurs (between 80 and 90 percent, according to a recent US study) run home-based businesses where, as specialists, their focus is more on personal professional development. They are more interested in increasing their skills in the goods and services they provide rather than on business and growth.[7]

You can see how business practices differ between a solo venture and one operated by an entrepreneur who intends to grow and eventually sell the business. It follows that the solopreneur mindset—their aspirations, objectives, and attitude towards being in business—also differ from that of entrepreneurs.

That's not all. As a solopreneur, if you don't do it, it doesn't get done. There's no one to delegate to. It's also difficult to separate your personal and business life; in fact, many don't see that as an objective because they are pursuing a passion that fulfills them as a person.

Many solopreneurs also report that it's an incredibly isolating experience. No staff, partners, or team are around to provide feedback or validation.

> The solopreneur's ability to scale a business tends to be limited because they are more focused on the idea and not so much on business growth.

Finally, because a solo business tends to be a low-cost higher-risk venture, solopreneurs are less likely to have access to financing through bank loans or even non-traditional lenders.[8]

Having a mentor who understands the special needs of the solopreneur can help you succeed.

SHOULD I SEEK A MENTOR?

If they do invest the time and energy into a mentoring relationship, solopreneurs worry if the return on that investment will be worth it. Will it distract from the 'real work' of running a business by yourself?

Not least, the psycho-emotional factor I alluded to in the introduction to this chapter may be at work: the fear of being seen as inadequate, somehow 'deficient,' not having 'the goods,' and exposing yourself to be a fraud, not really cut out for the business world. Sound familiar?

I hear this from solopreneurs all the time. They hear it from family, friends, acquaintances, even complete strangers: "What makes you think you can do this?"

The doubt creeps in, hangs on, and stays like a bad smell. They don't have a partner or a team or an entire corporation cheering for them. Often, they have no one at all.

There is no opposing voice saying, "Yes, you can! Let's dig down and find a way together!"

That's where the right mentor comes in.

WHAT CAN A MENTOR DO FOR YOU, THE SOLOPRENEUR?

The good news is that a lot of attention has recently been paid to mentorship generally and business mentorship specifically. Solid evidence is emerging that tells us that mentoring is critical for transformative development and growth, personally and professionally.

Let's look at some evidence.

I've already noted that a high percentage of small businesses fail within the first five years after starting up. The sad truth is that most small businesses fail within ten years, even if they survive the first five.

The main reason is that many business owners lack basic business competencies, especially about how to manage their finances. In fact, recent research indicates that this accounts for nearly half of all small business failures.[9]

Other studies discovered that many entrepreneurs—women in particular—lack confidence, fear failure, and have little firsthand knowledge about how to run a business.[10]

Mentoring by an experienced and successful individual means the difference between success and failure for many small business owners. Why? Because these seasoned professionals can assist you to recognize and address the major causes of business failure. They also help you develop the confidence to make decisions and learn from your mistakes.

The right mentor helps you recognize your strengths, allowing you to develop and grow into your role as an entrepreneur. They bring with them the insights that only experience can teach. The right mentor is not directive; they don't tell you what to do. They guide you so that you learn how to stand on your own.

You likely know how to work in your business, whether that is as a financial consultant, a craftsperson, an artist, a film maker, a marketer, or a social media consultant. But do you know how to work on your business? How to deal with day-to-day tasks such as:

Harness the Power of Mentoring 7

- Setting up and tracking your finances.
- Tracking inventory.
- Dealing with suppliers.
- Marketing and promoting your goods and services.
- Developing contracts for tasks you intend to outsource.
- Pursuing professional development.
- Continuously monitoring the business environment.
- And countless other details on the business side of what you offer.

As a successful solopreneur, your mentor will have had to master these tasks and more.

What your mentor *cannot* do for you is ensure that you will succeed. That's beyond anyone's power. But the right mentor will improve your odds of success by helping you identify what you need to know, what skills you need to have, and how to develop the capacity to be a successful entrepreneur.

As a solopreneur, however, you need to have a mentor who understands your mindset and the business practices that are important for a solopreneur to master. If your objective is to continuously improve your skill and knowledge rather than grow a business by hiring and delegating to employees, your mentor needs to know that.

A further and equally important part of the mentorship will be to discern just what type of an entrepreneur you are. We'll cover that in chapters 2 and 3.

MORE THAN GUIDANCE

I recently came across a newly-published book by Canadian uber-thinker Dan Pontefract: *Open to Think: Slow Down, Think Creatively and Make Better Decisions.*[11] He got me thinking.

I make my best decisions when I slow down and review the information and facts at hand in a new light. It isn't easy, but then when is something worthwhile ever a walk in the park? This is particularly true in today's frenetic world where information flies at us—and right by us—without cease.

When I read Dan's book, I came to the realization that this is why developmental mentoring is so powerful. With the right mentor, we stop tearing about. We put our tendency to Do-Do-Do on pause. We take time to dream, reflect, and think.

In those few hours that mentee and mentor spend together, they practice what Dan calls 'Open Thinking'. They co-create a space for "marinating in the moment, dreaming up ideas, and deciding what to do with them."[12]

Mentor and mentee thoughtfully mull over the evidence, consider the possibilities and consequences, and decide upon the best course of action.

With repetition through the many months of a mentorship, they rewire their capacity for thoughtful reflection and decision making. The quality of their thinking, as David Clutterbuck notes, becomes deeper.

WHEN IS THE RIGHT TIME TO HAVE A MENTOR?

Without being glib, any time is the right time. When you are starting something new, whether that is starting a new business venture or growing an existing one, a mentor is a good idea.

Why? You may be unsure of what steps to take or how to evaluate your progress. You may not know what options are available to you, or what resources you can tap into. You need an objective sounding board.

Harness the Power of Mentoring   9

When starting something new, it's not unusual to be uncertain, to lack confidence—after all, you've not gone down this path before! Your mentor can help you with many of the unknowns and help you learn to make decisions that are right for you and how to learn from your mistakes.

Remember, everyone makes mistakes. We don't learn if we don't. The important part of making mistakes is what did you learn from the experience? Your mentor can help you unpack that learning and figure out what it implies for you. For the solopreneur, this support can make the difference between success and failure.

In difficult economic times, starting a business or taking it in a different direction may seem counterintuitive. The fact is more people are becoming entrepreneurs—and even more are becoming solopreneurs—than ever before. Older workers, for example, are foregoing retirement to start new business ventures. I'm one of them!

Nelson Mandela famously said, "The most discouraging moments are precisely the time to launch an initiative." Really? Why would you start something new just when the stars seem to be aligned against you?

> Start with your vision. Know your strengths and use them to your advantage. Live your values, be open to change, and be proud of your roots. And never, ever, give up.
>
> **—Robert K. Irving**, president, Cavendish Farms.

Someone with a true entrepreneurial spirit, someone who is passionate about their entrepreneurial ambitions and dreams, sees opportunity instead of adversity. They can turn a dark time's energy into a positive force.

Having a mentor at such a time can help you keep that positive energy burning because you may be surrounded by negativity. A mentor who encourages you will help you keep up your momentum.

I've had a personal experience of just such a dark night of the soul. After a successful decade-long career as a senior advisor to a federal government agency, cutbacks meant that knowledge workers such as me were suddenly seen as disposable. Many years away from my planned retirement, I faced an uncertain future where I did not know how I would support my family.

I also suffered from the impending loss of my professional identity, built up over decades of my career, as a respected subject matter expert and leader.

I was fortunate to find mentors who helped me remember that I was more than just my position in a well-paid and prestigious job. They helped me remember that the reason I had achieved that position was because of my *intra*preneurial approach, my way of working with others, and the knowledge, skills, and expertise I'd developed—all transferable skills to the private sector.

I had what I needed to work *in* a business.

I reached out, asked for help, and was rewarded with the support of mentors who helped me fashion my ideas and strengths into reality: a consulting business for research, writing, and editing. They helped me see opportunities and options that, because of my relative inexperience in the business world, I wasn't aware of.

With the help of my mentors, I explored my options. I *knew* that establishing a business venture was something I really wanted.

Most importantly, my mentors also helped me learn how to work ON my business, that is, obtain the knowledge and skills that I needed so that I could be not just a superior researcher, writer, and editor, but a competent business owner too. That's made all the difference.

The other lesson I learned from my business mentors was how important it is to maintain momentum.

And never give up, say the leading successful entrepreneurs.

Never give up.

THE RIGHT MENTOR FOR A SOLOPRENEUR IS...

Someone who understands that solopreneurs have objectives, attitude, and a mindset that differs from other types of entrepreneurs.

The right mentor helps solopreneurs develop business practices that take these differences into account.

The right mentor encourages the mentee to practice Open Thinking: slow down, think creatively, and make better decisions.

Chapter 1: KEY INSIGHTS

1. Everyone can benefit from having a mentor, but solopreneurs benefit most of all in the business world. They are indeed 'special' (unique in a good way) with different business practices and mindset than other entrepreneurs. They face some challenges that other entrepreneurs don't encounter, at least not to the same degree.

2. Feeling inadequate is a common response to being overwhelmed by all the moving parts you encounter while trying to start or grow or even maintain a business. Without someone in your corner, there is no counterpoint to the naysayers.

3. People new to the business world often don't have firsthand experience in entrepreneurship, so they don't really know what business success is supposed to look like. Nor do they have the insight to know whether success is just around the corner (or not).

4. If you don't have an experienced partner or boss to help you work things out, how do you judge what is the right decision or strategy? Many solopreneurs say, "Well, I just make it up as I go along!" Since they haven't seen it, they find it challenging to be it. That's why the support of someone who has 'been there, done it' is so important—and crucial—to success.

5. The right mentor won't tell you what to do. They work

Harness the Power of Mentoring   13

hard, as do you, to develop a trusting and respectful relationship. They will challenge you, but above all will listen to you. They help you identify what you need to focus on, how to find the best solutions for you, and how to learn from your mistakes.

6. Practice Open Thinking every day. Create a space to slow down, think creatively. Deepen your thinking. It will be difficult at first but persevere. You will learn to make better decisions.

7. There is no 'right time' to work with a mentor, but a mentor is particularly helpful when you are starting something new, whether that's an entirely new business venture or an expansion of an existing one.

8. The support of a mentor can help you through the dark times when life throws you a curve. Don't be afraid to reach out but remember that it is up to you to persist. Don't get bogged down in 'what if.' You can never have a better past. Look to the future. Never give up.

9. You are likely quite good at what your business produces or provides as a service, otherwise why would you think you could make a living at it? So, you know how to work in your business. But do you know how to work on your business, that is, deal with cash flow, suppliers, marketing, etc.? Your mentor can help you identify blind spots and find out how to fill gaps to develop knowledge and skills for success.

Today mentoring has become collaborative; it is now a mutual discovery process in which both the mentor and mentee have something to bring to the relationship ("the give") and something to gain that broadens each of their perspectives ("the get"). Wisdom is not just passed down but discovered and nurtured. This shift frees both partners to learn together.

—Lois Zachary, internationally recognized expert on mentoring, author of *The Mentor's Guide and The Mentee's Guide.*

VIGNETTE – Jennifer's Story

I was so embarrassed as I met my mentor for the first time.

I was in a very difficult point in my life where I felt isolated, shaken, and fearful; I was hoping for clarity and confidence-building, but I knew nothing other than I needed to create income while learning to cope with new and serious health issues. I saw the business mentorship as a chance to 'shake up my luck.'

One of the key learning moments came early for me during that first meeting with my mentor. Our meetings were not private as my mentor was in a shared office space with his administrative assistant. My mentor's colleague asked me a personal question. I responded with a rudely blunt and honest answer.

It was then I realized I was looking for simple solutions to complex problems. As the mentorship unfolded, it gave me an opportunity to see myself in a new situation; in that awkward and cringey first meeting experience, I realized I needed to know there were people in my corner.

The mentorship got the ball rolling and kept me focused on a project towards a solopreneur career that helped me build a sense of productivity and empowerment after a time of having none. My confidence grew, and I learned how to assess business opportunities in my chosen industry: I wanted to establish a greenhouse operation supplying local grocers. I learned that it's a difficult way to make a living, so with my mentor I developed a plan to eventually get me where I wanted to be.

Now I have a registered business that will make money someday and an expanding clientele and service offerings. It is 180 degrees away from what I thought I would be doing at the beginning of my mentorship, but it reflects more of who I am, something I'm more aware of and comfortable with since my business mentorship.

LIST OF COMMONLY-USED TERMS IN THIS BOOK

MENTORING

Mentoring is a relationship where one or more persons reaches out for help, support, and guidance from another, more experienced individual. Mentoring can occur one-to-one, as a group, by peers, at distance (through the internet or phone), cross-generational, or in other forms. In a healthy mentoring relationship, both mentees and mentors learn, grow, and develop.

COACHING

Coaching is task oriented and often focuses on refining a skill such as public speaking, strategic thinking, athletic skills, etc. The coach helps the learner build up skills by teaching specific steps. The focus is generally short-term, and performance driven. For more on this topic, see Management Mentors' free white paper that discusses the complete list of differences between coaching and mentoring.

MENTOR

A mentor is a servant leader: authentic, engaging, trustworthy, humble yet confident, and willing to learn. A mentor offers the gift of experiences and expertise, is a good listener, and is willing to give time and energy to help others succeed without doling out advice or directives. A mentor is someone who helps others find their passion and learn to stand on their own.

MENTEE

A mentee is a person in a transition or someone who feels stalled or uncertain about the direction to take with their career; they are ready to reach out for help. A mentee seeks support and guidance to help them learn how to succeed. A mentee is not afraid to learn from mistakes nor to take the initiative. A mentee is willing to be open, honest, authentic, and trustworthy. They are ready to do the work required to succeed.

ENTREPRENEUR

An entrepreneur is someone who develops, launches, and runs a business venture. Entrepreneurs are both leaders and managers, and always innovators. In the classic sense, entrepreneurs typically start a business, find capital to finance it, and hire employees to work in the business. Entrepreneurs are risk-takers and risk managers.

SOLOPRENEUR

A solopreneur is a unique type of entrepreneur who is not focused on business growth so much as on excellence in the products or services they sell. As sole proprietors, solopreneurs choose to do the work themselves while outsourcing specific tasks such as accounting or marketing and devoting their energies to developing top-notch skills and services.

INTRAPRENEUR

An intrapreneur is an individual who acts like an entrepreneur while working for someone else. They apply the fundamental principles and strategies of entrepreneurship to their role within an organization.

18   Harness the Power of Mentoring

> Mentoring involves primarily listening with empathy, sharing experience and professional friendship, developing insight through reflection, being a sounding board, encouraging.
>
> **—David Clutterbuck**, author, researcher, and leading international mentoring expert.

2

Values, Purpose, Vision, and Goals

What do you want to achieve?

> If you can tune into your purpose and really align with it, setting goals so that your vision is an expression of that purpose, then life flows much more easily.
>
> **—Jack Canfield**, author of many books on success such as *Chicken Soup for the Soul* and *The Success Principles*™.

The decisions we make in life and work reflect our values and what we believe is our purpose in living. On that foundation, we develop a vision for the future we desire and goals to get us there.

What do you value most, and why? Let's take a pause in our very busy lives to think about that. This process of *discernment* is an important—critical—first step to prepare for a mentorship.

For some, family is the most valued part of their lives,

representing love, stability, personal history, belonging, and other emotions. For others, being appreciated and respected is most important because that validates their efforts.

Make a list of what you value and write down why each item matters to you. Then choose the top three or four that stand out as your top values.

WHY ARE YOU ON THIS EARTH?

Finding our purpose—or purposes— in life requires deep searching within ourselves. We need to look for the meaning in our existence. Heady stuff!

In his powerful book *Man's Search for Meaning*,[14] Holocaust survivor Viktor Frankl chronicles his search to find meaning and the will to *be* in even the most desperate of situations. He concludes that we don't create meaning; we discover it.

Indigenous Elder Dr. Joseph Couture[15] observed, "You have all the answers within you." He once said to me, "There is within me a voice that tells me who I am and where I am." In a busy, noisy world, hearing that voice can be a challenge. Can you hear it?

You can do this in your own life by finding a quiet space and asking yourself a few simple—but profound—questions:

- What is the meaning of your life?

- Why are you here?

- What is your purpose in living?

I struggled with these questions for a long time. Then I realized that everything I did that I really enjoyed—and got the most fulfillment from—seemed to have a common theme. These were the moments in which I helped others rise to new heights and realize their true potential. The meaning and purpose of my life became clear.

DISCOVER YOUR PURPOSE

Jack Canfield, the originator of the *Chicken Soup for the Soul*® series[16], suggests the following four steps to discover your purpose(s):

1. First, he says, what do you love to do? What comes easily to you?

2. Then, he says, identify the two qualities you most enjoy expressing: creativity? finishing a project? love? Jack asks you to describe how you express these qualities every day: What do you do? Write? Paint? Inspire others? Support those in need? Design new solutions to problems?

3. Next, write a description of your perfect world. Think of it this way: A spiritual being landed on the earth and said that tomorrow is the day that will be most perfect in this world. What would that day look like to you?

Now combine steps one to three and write your personal purpose statement. As an example, here's what Jack Canfield says on his website is his purpose in life:

Inspiring and empowering people to live their highest vision in a context of love and joy.

LISTEN TO YOUR HEART

The next step is to discover what your heart is telling you to do. Remember Viktor Frankl and Joseph Couture's advice: it's really within you to discover.

Where do you see yourself in one, three, and ten years from now? What does your personal and professional life look like?

Be specific. Be detailed. Describe what your relationships, your finances, your successes, and your happiness would be like if your life were perfect. Envision what your living space would look like: Can you see the sun shining through the window on your favorite chair? Can you see yourself relaxing there, listening to your favorite music?

Don't let negative or skeptical thoughts creep in. Write down your vision. Studies show clearly that we're more likely to act on what we write down. The act of writing will also help you slow down and really explore your inner world.

WHAT IS YOUR PURPOSE IN LIFE?

Now set this aside for a while, then come back later with fresh eyes to review what you've written.

Do you see what your purpose is in this life? Why you exist on this planet? It may take some further pondering, or it may leap off the page. If you understand yourself and your purpose in living, I believe you will be able to lead a more satisfying, productive, and coherent life doing what you enjoy and, in turn, will be inspired to help others along the way.

For example, when I first completed this exercise, I was at a loss to explain my purpose in living. It seemed to be too enormous to pin down! As the years unfolded, I kept coming back to it.

Now, I keep what I feel is my purpose in front of me at all times. I write it into my business mission and vision statement: What gives me joy is helping others rise to new heights and reach their full potential.

I realized that was why, as an addictions expert, I focused on the healing rather than the beginning of addictive behavior. I was more interested in how people got out of a mess than how they got into it in the first place.

That self-knowledge helped me understand better how and why I undertook certain projects. In writing these books and other information products I hope to help solopreneurs get the help they need.

My vision for this book is that solopreneurs will learn to be active co-creators with their mentors. Together, they will create supportive environment and nurture healthy mentoring relationships that will pay dividends for years to come.

I wrote my purpose into the business mission and vision for *The Business Mentoring Solution* series. I determined that the guiding principle for this venture—my North Star—is *Support Solopreneur Success*. I achieve this by contributing to supportive environments and nurturing healthy relationships. My mission statement is shown below.

Try this exercise yourself and see if you can write a mission and vision statement for your solopreneur business. What are *your* guiding principles? What is *your* North Star?

The Business Mentoring Solution: Mission Statement

To help solopreneurs rise to new heights
and realize their true potential.

SET YOUR SIGHTS ON THE HORIZON

It's time to get concrete.

Based on your values, vision, and purpose, what do you need and want to accomplish over the next 12 months?

What do you need to do (and think) to make that happen?

What are your goals?

> "Yes, but…I don't have the skills, experience, finances, etc. to do that!"

Here's a tip:

Act as if you do.

Remember that we usually get what we expect. Just do it—take a leap of faith. Figure it out along the way. If you don't change what you are doing, how can you possibly expect different results? What do you stand to lose? At worst, you will still be where you were before you tried something different.

Make a plan with specific actions and dates and tell someone else about it.

Ask them to check in on your progress at regular intervals as your accountability partner. You are more likely to stop procrastinating if you are accountable to someone else.

The planner/journal that accompanies this book includes exercises to help you complete this process. It will help you write your purpose in living into your business mission and vision.

THE RIGHT MENTOR FOR A SOLOPRENEUR IS...

Someone who helps you:

- Explore your values,
- Identify your purpose,
- See your vision,
- Find your North Star,
- Set realistic goals.

The right mentor does not tell you what to do, nor do they dole out advice.

Instead, they lead you to learn how to think more deeply, learn from your mistakes, and develop confidence.

Chapter 2: KEY INSIGHTS

1. Identify what is most important to you—what you value and why.
2. What do you want your life (personal and professional) to look like in a few years?
3. Discovering your purpose(s) in life can take some work. Remember that you have everything you need within you to discover your purpose in life. It takes a little effort and courage to pull it out into the light.
4. Start by examining what you love to do and what comes easily to you (even if it's easy because you practiced a lot).
5. What qualities do you love to express daily? How do you express them? How do these qualities translate into your guiding principles, i.e., your North Star, that keeps you pointed in the right direction?
6. What would your perfect world look like? If, on a scale of one to ten, your perfect world is a ten, but you are at three right now, what would it take to be at four? Then five? Then six? And so on?
7. Now combine these three steps into a personal purpose statement that expresses what gives you joy, how you enact those qualities, and what world you will create in the process.
8. Decide what you will achieve over the next 12 months and what you need to do to accomplish that goal. Commit to action. Discourage negative thoughts. Act as if you were already well on your way. Just do it.

9. Write your purpose in living into your business mission and vision statements.

> So many of us, myself included, live important aspects of our lives with the silent mantra of "I'll believe it when I see it" and in doing so we hold ourselves back, limit what's possible, and negate the power of our mind, imagination, and intention to allow and create things, situations, experiences, and outcomes that are new, unpredictable, and even miraculous.
>
> —**Mike Robbins**, motivational speaker and author of *Focus on the Good Stuff* and *Be Yourself, Everyone Else is Already Taken.*

VIGNETTE – Margaret's story

I really struggled with clarifying what I wanted to be and do—I'd spent so much of my life trying to meet everyone else's expectations that I'd lost sight of my own needs and desires. With my mentor's encouragement, I undertook a fearless personal inventory.

When I really thought about what was important to ME, what I loved to do, what seemed effortless, and thought about the qualities that I try to express, my purpose became clearer. I realized that actively working towards a better world, for social justice, was what I wanted and needed to do. It's what fires me up and I'm good at it.

So, I set my goal for the next 12 months towards establishing a social enterprise that will help local farmers develop new markets for their produce. This venture will also help get healthy, locally-produced foods into schools.

I don't know how to do it yet—there are lots of details to work out—but I will figure it out.

With my mentor's help.

3

Doing an Inventory

Discover what you need NOW

> The real voyage of discovery consists not in seeing new landscapes but in having new eyes.
>
> **—Marcel Proust**, French writer.

Now that you have a good sense of your values, your purpose, your vision, and what you want to achieve, it's time to do an honest inventory of where you are *now*. That discovery will help you figure out what you need to do to get to the next step. Then the next. And so on.

It's time to take stock. What are you prepared to do—emotionally, financially, physically—to make your business dreams a reality? Are you ready to take it on?

Remember that, as a solopreneur, your attitude, objectives, and mindset are different from those of other entrepreneurs. When you take inspiration from others, check where they are coming from: Is it in line with your vision?

A PERSONAL INVENTORY

If you build on your strengths when you start a business rather than on something you know little about, you are more likely to succeed. That's because you will be able to get started *doing* rather than *learning*. If you know how to work IN your business, you will have more time and energy to devote to working ON your business.

Take a few minutes and answer the following questions as honestly as possible (see the relevant section in the planner/journal that accompanies this book):

- What are you really good at and what do you enjoy doing?

- What are you most experienced at doing?

- What credentials or technical skills do you have?

- What other credentials or technical skills will you need?

- Do you have contacts in this industry or sector?

- Do you have access to certain key resources, particularly those that your competitors do not have?

Will you need to develop your soft skills as well? *Soft skills* is the term applied to nontechnical expertise that you might learn in a Dale Carnegie course on how to build relationships with other people. Are you a friendly person who can easily develop rapport with others? Can you win others to your way of thinking? Can you manage conflict in a positive way?

Connecting and building relationships with others is a critical business skill. American business consultant Suzanne Evans says business never gets done in your house, so prepare to get out to where colleagues and prospects hang out.[17]

Why? Suzanne notes that the messages you need to send to promote your business never get crafted in a messaging program or through message coaching. They get crafted in conversations.

You will simply have to get out and meet people. You will need to talk to them, address their pain point—the problem that your product or service will solve for your customers or clients—and suggest a solution that they can see is of value to them.

And you need to do it in a unique way.

If you are unsure about your ability to develop relationships with those who may buy your product or service, you might need to brush up on your people skills. Your mentor may be able to help you practice and develop a style that works for you.

YOUR TIME COMMITMENT

There's an old saying in entrepreneurial circles: If you aren't making money, it's not a business; it's a hobby.

What does it take to make money? In addition to being certain that what you are selling is what people want to buy, you need to make sure that you can commit the time and energy it takes to make a business succeed.

Be realistic. Your business venture won't work if your personal life falls apart around you. Schedule time for the non-work parts of your life and strive for harmony and balance. Remember to look after yourself and those who are important to you so that you can better deal with the stresses of running your business.

YOUR FINANCIAL COMMITMENT

In addition to family, friends, and fools, most small businesses are launched with the entrepreneur's own money. Most often, the business is started while the owner still has sufficient income from other sources to keep the wheels on their bus until the business concept is shown to be successful.

The Dragons' Den™ TV show producers suggest that you exercise extreme caution in staking your personal finances in your business. In other words, be careful about spending your own money to develop a product or service. They advise structuring your personal finances in *wealth buckets*: living expenses, emergency funds, major assets, education funds, retirement funds, and net worth.[18]

The wealth buckets are explained further in the diagram on the next page of this book.

Examine each of these buckets and assess how well you have filled them. What do you need to work on?

Remember to draw a line to indicate when and under what circumstances you will just walk away from the business.

What would be the signs that you should do this?

This is where your mentor can provide valuable insight.

YOUR PERSONALITY

To be a successful solopreneur, you will need to know yourself very well, as well, if not better than you know your business prospects. You can't undergo a personality transplant when you start a new business. You *can* do an honest personal inventory to avoid being your own worst enemy.

Writing in Forbes online business magazine, John Rampton identified five common personality traits possessed by entrepreneurs:[19]

- Passion (driven by heart).

- Resilience (able to rise from failure).

- Strong sense of self (self-confident and self-motivated).

- Flexibility (able to adapt to changes and challenges).

- Vision (can see the future before it happens).

Three other aspects of your personality to examine are your risk tolerance, your work style, and how you deal with problems.

WEALTH BUCKETS

Living expenses: Cut back as much as possible on what you don't really need.

Emergency funds: You should have six to 12 months of funds in reserve before leaving your paying job.

Major assets: Postpone major expenses until your business' cash flow is established.

Education funds: Don't be tempted! Hands off! Leave your children's education funds alone.

Retirement funds: Similarly, leave any retirement funds alone. Reserve 15 percent of the income you draw from your business for your retirement fund.

Net worth: Don't risk more than five to 15 percent of your total net worth. Instead, draw on other resources such as a bank loan.

Risk tolerance: If you have RRSPs or other investments, you are likely familiar with your bank's process of assessing how much risk you are willing to bear. They help you choose an investment strategy that matches your risk tolerance level, so you can sleep at night.

For example, an aggressive strategy works for some, while others prefer a more balanced or even conservative approach to investment. It also depends on circumstances in your life such as age, dependents, and other factors.

It's a given that anyone in business must take some degree of risk. But a successful business owner is someone who knows how to *manage* risk well.

The accompanying planner/journal presents a simple approach to develop a risk management strategy that suits your preferred style.

Work style: Think about how you work best. Do you need to do it all yourself or do you find others to fill in the gaps?

Solopreneurs often try to do it all themselves—be truthful about what you can and cannot handle at this point. Do you need a bookkeeper or a social media consultant?

Are you good at leading others and delegating work so that it gets done? Are you a micromanager? Or do you prefer to do it yourself (the mark of a true solopreneur).

Dealing with problems: Being a solopreneur means you are going to have make decisions all the time by yourself and navigate the speed bumps you will encounter. Do you tend to avoid problems or solve them?

- If you are a problem solver, do you find yourself down rabbit holes or putting out fires day in, day out? How can you avoid falling into these traps?

Harness the Power of Mentoring   35

- If you tend to avoid problems, look out! That's a dangerous practice. Make sure you find someone to help you deal with challenges that arise.

A mentor is the perfect solution to help you deal with problems in a healthy, productive way. They can help you see your blind spots and develop a strategy that works for you, the solopreneur.

REACHING OUT

Whatever you bring to your business emotionally, financially, personally, and in terms of time and energy, knowing when to reach out is critical. It's particularly important for a solopreneur. You don't have a team of people working in your business; you need to create that team around you.

Seek the support of family and friends *if* that support is sincere, honest, and arises from their genuine interest in your wellbeing.

Set up an advisory board of successful solopreneurs— people who 'get' your attitude, vision, and mindset—who will help you through the process of launching your business and surviving the early years. Enlist the support of people who understand the business practices that fit best with your attitude, vision, and objectives.

Better yet, find yourself a business mentor!

The next chapter will help you find the right mentor for you, the solopreneur.

...[T]he mentoring process doesn't begin with you and your mentor; it begins with you. Before you can engage with a mentor, you need to do some serious and focused preparation that will help you know better what you want to achieve, how you learn best, and what kind of mentoring relationship might work well for you.

—**Lois Zachary**, *The Mentee's Guide*, 2009, p. 15.

THE RIGHT MENTOR FOR A SOLOPRENEUR IS...

Someone who will help you identify not only your weaknesses and gaps but also your strengths and passions; who will strive to understand what you want to achieve, how you learn, and what kind of a relationship will be most effective.

They help you accurately assess your commitments and your financial situation.

The right mentor helps you learn to deal with problems and make the best decisions for your personality type.

Chapter 3: KEY INSIGHTS

1. Conduct an honest inventory of your strengths and limitations.
2. Build on your strengths so that you can concentrate on action rather than on learning too many new things.
3. List your credentials or technical skills. Identify what additional credentials or technical skills you need. List the inroads you already have in the industry or sector.
4. Assess your soft skills. Get out of your office and into the community. Remember that your core messages will only be honed through conversations with others.
5. Ensure that your work, personal, and family times are in harmony.
6. Don't quit your day job until you are certain that you can afford to do so. Set up a system of wealth buckets. Don't risk your savings.
7. Know your personality. How well can you tolerate risk and how do you manage risk? How do you work with others? What's your problem-solving style?
8. Reach out. You can't run the world by yourself.

> Don't be afraid to ask questions. Don't be afraid to ask for help when you need it. I do that every day.
>
> Asking for help isn't a sign of weakness, it's a sign of strength. It shows you have the courage to admit when you don't know something, and then allows you to learn something new.
>
> **—Barack Obama**, 44th US President.

VIGNETTE – Patricia's Story

I'm an artist—a photographer specializing in landscapes and culture-scapes. I joined a business mentoring program to help me develop my business concept. I was shocked to learn that I was matched with a mentor who was an accountant! I mean, I'm an artist!

But what I found out was that having an accountant as a mentor was just what I needed at that time. I had no idea how to set up and manage the financial part of my business. He helped me understand that part and solved some tax issues for me too.

Once I did the math, I figured out that selling big canvases wasn't as profitable as I'd hoped, and I had to deal with galleries and buy materials for making the canvases and shipping them. That meant that I had to lay out a lot of money in advance. My smaller products, such as cards, are less expensive and very popular. So, I revised my original business plan to focus more on the smaller products.

I'm glad I listened to my mentor. If I hadn't calculated the cash flow projections, I would continue to struggle with my finances.

I learned that to be a successful solopreneur, I had to learn how to work *on*, not just *in*, my business, and that it's critical to reach out for help.

4

The Right Mentor for You

Finding the best fit for a solopreneur

> Today mentoring has become collaborative. It is now a mutual discovery process in which both mentor and mentee have something to bring to the relationship ("the give") and something to gain that broadens each of their perspectives ("the get").
>
> **—Lois J. Zachary,** *The Mentor's Guide,* 2012, p.3.

The mentoring relationship used to be all about an older, wiser, more experienced person taking a protégé under their wing and making things happen for them. No longer.

The New Wave of mentoring is all about a mutually respectful relationship, says leading mentoring expert David Clutterbuck, where the mentor helps the mentee deepen

42   Harness the Power of Mentoring

their thinking and hone their ability to make decisions that will work for them.

In turn, the mentor benefits from new thinking, new insights, and the honest joy of helping another succeed. A mentoring relationship goes both ways. Ideally, both mentor and mentee will benefit.

A recent mentor I know observed that, "Being a mentor caused me to question some of the habits I'd fallen into as an entrepreneur. My mentee's questions caused me to rethink and develop new, more effective strategies for my own business."

Your work of getting to know yourself is almost done, but not quite. There are a few other steps to take in your self-examination:

• Why do you think you need a mentor?

• What do you need, want, and expect?

• What kind of relationship would help you best?

DO YOU HAVE WHAT IT TAKES TO BE MENTORED?

Take a good hard look at yourself. Are you, the mentee, ready to be mentored? You may want to review this list with someone who knows you well.

• Are you open and flexible, ready to change what you do and how you approach issues?

• Are you resilient, ready to take reasonable leaps and learn from your mistakes?

• Are you ready to be challenged?

• Are you eager and committed to learning?

4

The Right Mentor for You

Finding the best fit for a solopreneur

> Today mentoring has become collaborative. It is now a mutual discovery process in which both mentor and mentee have something to bring to the relationship ("the give") and something to gain that broadens each of their perspectives ("the get").
>
> —**Lois J. Zachary,** *The Mentor's Guide,* 2012, p.3.

The mentoring relationship used to be all about an older, wiser, more experienced person taking a protégé under their wing and making things happen for them. No longer.

The New Wave of mentoring is all about a mutually respectful relationship, says leading mentoring expert David Clutterbuck, where the mentor helps the mentee deepen

42   Harness the Power of Mentoring

their thinking and hone their ability to make decisions that will work for them.

In turn, the mentor benefits from new thinking, new insights, and the honest joy of helping another succeed. A mentoring relationship goes both ways. Ideally, both mentor and mentee will benefit.

A recent mentor I know observed that, "Being a mentor caused me to question some of the habits I'd fallen into as an entrepreneur. My mentee's questions caused me to rethink and develop new, more effective strategies for my own business."

Your work of getting to know yourself is almost done, but not quite. There are a few other steps to take in your self-examination:

- Why do you think you need a mentor?

- What do you need, want, and expect?

- What kind of relationship would help you best?

DO YOU HAVE WHAT IT TAKES TO BE MENTORED?

Take a good hard look at yourself. Are you, the mentee, ready to be mentored? You may want to review this list with someone who knows you well.

- Are you open and flexible, ready to change what you do and how you approach issues?

- Are you resilient, ready to take reasonable leaps and learn from your mistakes?

- Are you ready to be challenged?

- Are you eager and committed to learning?

WHAT MAKES A GREAT MENTOR?

Studies tell us that great mentors—the ones who facilitate positive, transformative change in others—don't tell you what to do. Rather, they help you develop as a person and a business owner.

Expect to be asked tough questions and be challenged. Above all, expect to be listened to and learn from their stories about being an entrepreneur.

What makes a great mentor for one person might be exactly wrong for someone else. If you don't feel the love, perhaps that's not the right person for you. BUT if you are feeling uncomfortable because you are being challenged, perhaps the fit is just right.

A word of caution: unless we have third party doing the matching (as in a formal mentoring program), we tend to choose people who are most like ourselves.

That's human nature. That person is not likely the best mentor for you.

FINDING THE RIGHT MENTOR FOR YOU

The easiest way to find a mentor is through a mentoring program that has protocols and screening tools to provide you with the best match to your needs.

As a solopreneur, you will not likely have access to such a program without paying a lot of money for the service—and that extra cash can be a scarce commodity as you start up a new business enterprise.

What are your options? First, forget about the big names. They are likely too busy to be of much good to you even if they agree, which is unlikely.

Second, look around locally. Who do you know, respect, and admire who has relevant experience? Do your homework. Who are the members of the local chamber of commerce, business associations, or are involved with other organizations such as Junior Achievement?

Check their LinkedIn profiles, Twitter feeds, Facebook pages, and other social media. Search for a company profile.

Now reach out, but gently.

Develop a connection with the individual that you are looking at as a potential mentor. You don't want to come across as a stalker or be too pushy.

Comment positively on their posts, Retweet one of their tweets, invite them to join your LinkedIn network (with a personal note).

Remember that you are trying to establish if this individual would be a good fit for you at this time.

WHEN YOU THINK YOU'VE FOUND THE RIGHT MENTOR... WHAT NEXT?

When you find someone with whom you believe you can develop an effective mentoring relationship, start with small talk. Ask about their interests and experience. How did they get to where they are now in their business?

It's a simple principle. If you talk about *their* interests, are genuinely interested in *them*, encourage them to talk about *themselves*, actively listen to what *they* have to say, and are friendly, sincere, and honestly appreciative...you may find a willing mentor.

By the way, a mentor shouldn't be looking for either financial compensation or a piece of your business. That's a definite flag that they aren't the right person for you.[20]

The right mentor is someone who wants to give back to the community. If you opt for a formally structured mentoring program offered by an organization such as the Forum for Women Entrepreneurs,[21] the mentors are usually volunteers and the mentees *may* pay a fee to the organization running the program.

In other programs (e.g., the Cherie Blair Foundation for Women[22]), no fee is applied. See the Appendix for further information.

The planner/journal that accompanies this book will help you plan a strategy and navigate the steps to find your mentor. It will help you keep organized and mindful during this important process.

WHAT TERMS SHOULD YOU SUGGEST TO A POTENTIAL MENTOR?

In a mentoring relationship, the mentee does the work. The mentor's job is to listen carefully, prompt you for more information, ask reflective questions to encourage you to go deeper, suggest alternatives, and challenge your assumptions and decisions.

We've found—and others' experiences confirm this—that mentoring can be effective when meetings are held once a month for about an hour. Your first get to know each other meeting may be longer, but one hour seems to be the perfect length for subsequent meetings.

One year is the usual length of time for a mentorship, but you and your mentor may decide to a) continue longer, or b) end earlier if your work together seems to have come to a reasonable conclusion.

Most mentors will see this as doable, particularly since they will not be expected to do much preparation for the meetings. They are to bring their experience and expertise to the table.

As a suggestion, demonstrate—don't just tell—your mentor that you are willing to do the work in this relationship:

- Show up on time.
- Be prepared.
- Have an agenda.
- Take responsibility for the meeting.
- Be accountable for developing action steps.

> Prospective mentees: be brave. When you ask someone to mentor you, the worst that can happen is that you break even. If the person says no, you didn't have a mentor before, anyway!
>
> **—Ken Blanchard & Claire Diaz-Ortiz**, authors, *One Minute Mentoring*, 2017, p.45.

THE RIGHT MENTOR FOR A SOLOPRENEUR IS...

Someone who is a good listener, challenges you, but doesn't dole out advice.

They help you explore options and develop connections across the business community.

They help you mature in your thinking and ability to assess situations and make the right decisions for *you*.

Chapter 4: KEY INSIGHTS

1. Examine why you need a mentor, what you expect, and the role that mentor will play.

2. Ensure that you are ready to be mentored: open, flexible, resilient, ready for change and to be challenged, committed, and eager to learn.

3. Look for a developmental mentoring experience where you will grow as a person and as a solopreneur.

4. Look locally for a mentor. Find someone you admire, respect, and has relevant experience. Do your homework.

5. Reach out gently. Establish a connection before you try to develop a relationship.

6. A mentor should not be looking for either compensation or a stake in your business.

VIGNETTE – John's story

I really didn't know where to start. I thought about the people who had been important influencers in my life—teachers, coaches, neighbors, Scout leaders—and thought long and hard about what I believed I needed to get out of mentoring at this point in my business.

I was still in the first year of startup and was uncertain about how and when to make the decision to leave my salaried job—which I hate—and take the plunge to work on my social media business full-time. I needed guidance.

I did some homework on local successful solopreneurs and found a couple who sounded interesting. I met one of them at a business mixer organized by the local chamber of commerce by asking a friend to introduce me.

I remembered that I didn't want to scare this potential mentor away, so I just expressed interest in her and her business story. I let her talk. It was easy being genuinely interested because she had accomplished so much.

I asked if I could have 15 minutes of her time within the next month or so to ask her some questions about my situation that I thought she might have some insights into. To my surprise, she agreed.

After our meeting, I asked if we could follow up with another, and she once again agreed. Then, to my surprise, she suggested that she would be pleased to mentor me and would meet with me once a month for an hour. She views this as 'giving back' because of the help she received from a mentor in her early years.

50 Harness the Power of Mentoring

I've learned a lot, and so has my mentor. I've survived my first year as a solopreneur and have plans—a definite date—by which I will leave my employer and commit to running my business full-time. I feel ready.

5

Working with Your Mentor

How to develop and nurture a healthy mentoring relationship

> A good mentor is a gift from the universe.
>
> **—Rajesh Setty,** author and entrepreneur

No magic formula exists for the perfect mentoring relationship. Rather, the factors that develop and maintain a healthy, effective mentoring relationship are common across most human relationships that work well.

Let's start with the outcomes you desire. You've completed your personal and professional inventory, so you have a fairly good handle on what you need from your mentor—although be prepared for unexpected insights as the relationship develops.

Do you have confidence issues? Are you lacking in knowledge and experience around marketing or finances?

52   Harness the Power of Mentoring

Unsure how to conduct and understand the results of a competitor analysis?

Most importantly, are you passionate about starting or growing your business? Does your mentor inspire you to do better?

Your mentor doesn't necessarily need to be experienced in your particular business area. One of my mentees through the Forum for Women Entrepreneurs mentoring program is a newcomer to Canada She was struggling to understand Canadian business communication styles, which were quite different from her home country's norms. I helped her understand why she was getting frustrated and how to figure out what was appropriate in different contexts. It's a critical part of doing business.

It can be helpful to have a mentor who works in your specific industry or sector if, for example, you wish to start an Etsy business and need to understand how that sector works. Access to insider expertise is necessary for setting up an Etsy business.

THE KEY FACTORS IN HEALTHY MENTORING RELATIONSHIPS

Let's take a closer look at what is known about mentoring relationships that work well for both mentor and mentee. This is what studies tell us a healthy mentoring relationship looks like:

1. Experience as a successful entrepreneur is an essential quality in a mentor but this needs to be accompanied by a healthy dose of humility. Arrogance has no place in this relationship. Your mentor should be confident because they have clear insight into what led to their success.

2. Research suggests that in a mentoring relationship that works, you and your mentor must be able to set clear goals and challenges. You need to identify milestones along the way so that you can benchmark your progress.

Harness the Power of Mentoring   53

3. Remember that a solopreneur's business practices, attitudes, and vision differ from that of a serial entrepreneur. Ensure that your mentor understands and 'gets' where you are coming from, particularly if he or she has a more conventional entrepreneurial mindset.

4. Communication is key. Your mentor needs to be a good listener—and so do you! A mentor should engage in reflective listening. That means you will hear your mentor paraphrase what you have said and ask you what you think you should do, something like this: "So I hear you say that you aren't sure about the size of the potential market for your widget? How can you find out?"

   That gives you the opportunity to either correct a misunderstanding or to expand on what the issue really means for you: "Yes, that's it exactly! I'm not sure if I should be considering a local market or whether it's better to develop a larger distribution system at this time."

5. Focus on your personal and professional development. As leading mentoring expert David Clutterbuck puts it, your mentor should be able to help you expand your ability to think through key decisions.

   This means your mentor shouldn't dole out advice nor should your mentor solve problems for you; you will learn how to do that yourself in a healthy mentoring relationship.

   You and your mentor are independent but collaborative learners.

6. Networking is another way that your mentor should be able to support your development as a solopreneur. Their connections will help you in your personal and professional development as they introduce you to members of their networks.

7. Your mentor should be a positive role model for you: "You need to *see* it to *be* it." In other words, if you don't know

what a successful solopreneur looks like, or what the life of a solopreneur is like, how can you aspire to be one? With your mentor's help, seek out and become acquainted with a network of solopreneurs. Watch and learn.

8.   Mutual benefit is another characteristic of a healthy mentoring relationship. Your mentor should derive some good from working with you.

One mentor expressed the benefit he received in this way: "I found that I was becoming better at my business because I was consciously examining why I made certain decisions so that I could in turn help my mentee do the same."

9.   Respect, honesty, and trust are key factors in any healthy relationship. They are expressed in several ways: being punctual, being prepared, being courteous, being truthful, maintaining confidentiality, and so on.

In other words, care for one another's wellbeing and ensure that the relationship is working well for each of you.

10.   Your mentor will nudge you out of your comfort zone. Yes, that's right. Be prepared to be uncomfortable.

In a healthy learning mentoring relationship, there is trust. Your mentor will encourage you to consider new options, try new approaches, develop new strategies, and learn from your errors or failures.

11.   In a healthy mentoring relationship, your mentor can challenge your thinking without you becoming defensive. You will find that becomes easier as your confidence grows.

12.   Your mentor should stay out of the weeds unless something terrible is about to happen if they don't intervene. Their role is not to micromanage your business, but to provide you with a view from the balcony.

Harness the Power of Mentoring   55

13. Finally, commitment is essential if this is going to work. That means commitment by you AND by your mentor to the mentoring relationship. Be on time. Be prepared. Follow through.

As in every other relationship, you and your mentor will need to be mindful about your work together.

Pay close attention, continuously evaluate the mentorship, and correct the course of your mentorship if necessary.

MAKE YOUR MENTORING RELATIONSHIP WORK

Your mentoring relationship takes work. Be mindful and present in your interactions with your mentor.

Take a few minutes at the end of each mentoring meeting to review with your mentor what you did together. What worked for you and why? What didn't work and why not? This is a time to exercise the respect, honesty, and trust factors so you can make the adjustments to your relationship that will help you keep on track to achieve your goals.

Refer to your personal inventory, mission, and vision.

Are you consistent?

Do you need to rethink the foundational elements?

IS THIS REALLY THE RIGHT PATH FOR ME?

During your mentorship, you may discover that you aren't ready to be an entrepreneur, let alone a solopreneur.

Carol Roth, the best-selling author of *The Entrepreneur Equation*,[23] states that it's not *"Could* I be an entrepreneur?" but *"Should* I be an entrepreneur now or ever?"

I would add that the next question for you is: "Should I be a *solopreneur* (at this time or ever)?"

This is an important reality check that should be on your agenda for the first few meetings with your mentor. If you are

56   Harness the Power of Mentoring

better suited to working with others in a partnership than working on your own to make a business succeed, so be it. If you are better suited to working for someone else, it's best to know early in the game.

But if being a solopreneur is the right fit, you need to confirm that fact before you go too far down the road. You and your mentor need to have a clear, mutually understood vision of what you wish to accomplish and whether that is realistic.

THE RIGHT MENTOR FOR A SOLOPRENEUR IS...

Someone who is collaborative but not directive in their approach to mentoring, respectful, honest, and trustworthy, but not afraid to challenge you and nudge you out of your comfort zone.

They help you decide if being a solopreneur, or even a conventional entrepreneur, is the right choice for you.

Ultimately, the right mentors get as much from the relationship as they put into it.

Chapter 5: KEY INSIGHTS

1. As in any healthy relationship, mentoring will take passion, commitment, dedication, and work.

2. Experience on the part of your mentor is essential, but so is your insight into your needs. What do you want to achieve? Develop clear goals and measure your progress.

3. Clear two-way communication is another key factor. Learn to really listen and express yourself clearly.

4. Remember that networking will introduce you to new ways of seeing and new opportunities. It will help you to grow as you interact with other, more experienced entrepreneurs you will meet via your mentor.

5. Exercise respect, honesty, and trust. When you are challenged and nudged out of your comfort zone—as you should be—these factors will help you rise to the challenge and become a better person.

6. Treat your mentoring relationship with the commitment and passion it deserves. Nurture it and it will serve you and your mentor well.

7. Commit to an honest exploration with your mentor about whether entrepreneurship, particularly being a solopreneur, is the best choice for you now or ever.

Be honest about what you personally need in a relationship…An honest discussion about expectations for the relationship is also critical.

This means explicitly asking your mentoring partner what she wants, needs, and expects out of the relationship and stating exactly what you want, need, and expect as well.

—Lois J. Zachary, author and internationally recognized expert on mentoring.

VIGNETTE – Alicia's story

I was amazed at how well John listened to me. He asked probing questions and mentioned issues that I hadn't considered before. Then he got out his calculator and showed me how to do a proper market analysis.

I learned from my mentor's challenges and nudges that my original business idea just wouldn't work for several very good reasons. I simply wouldn't be able to become profitable, even with hard work. The market just wasn't there.

I decided to give up on that idea and find a business that could have a real future.

I was disappointed and resistant at first to the fact that my original idea wasn't feasible, but I gained useful knowledge and learned new business skills.

I also learned that many business ideas won't work and that's OK. What is important is to be able to discern that and move on.

With my mentor's support, that's just what I did.

6

Fail to Plan, Plan to Fail

Create a strategy for solopreneur success

> Give me six hours to cut down the tree and I will use four to sharpen the axe.
>
> **—Abraham Lincoln**, 16th US President.

In this chapter, we'll look at two types of plans: a mentoring plan and a business plan. Let's start with developing a plan for your mentorship.

YOUR MENTORING PLAN

A mentoring plan is a map for your mentoring journey. It sets out goals and a schedule (timeline) for completion, but that's not all.

A mentoring plan should also:

- Break the process down into manageable stages.
- Clarify how you will measure success along the way.

62 Harness the Power of Mentoring

- Identify tasks to accomplish.
- Highlights points where you should pat yourself on the back.

BEGIN AT THE BEGINNING

First, reflect on what you want to accomplish from chapters two and three.

- What's your goal for this mentorship?
- Do you want to reach a certain stage in your business development?
- Learn critical skills?
- Or something else?

Now decide on what kind of mentoring is best for you and will help you reach your goal. Mentoring is most often one-on-one, but peer mentoring is powerful, and group or team mentoring works too.

For example, a group of First Nations (Mi'kmaq) women entrepreneurs in Prince Edward Island set up a mentoring circle, mirroring traditional support processes with both experienced entrepreneurs and Indigenous Elders present.

You can also combine different mentoring models, for example, peer mentoring and one-on-one mentoring. The options are only limited by your imagination and by what you feel would best meet your needs.

Don't forget that with modern technology such as Skype, Zoom, or Google Hangout, you can enjoy a productive mentoring relationship with a mentor from the other side of the world. The Cherie Blair Foundation for Women's Business Mentoring Programme (sic) works on this type of model (see the Appendix for more information and link to the website).

WHAT STEPS DO YOU NEED TO TAKE TO ACCOMPLISH YOUR GOALS?

The planner/journal that complements this book provides templates to help you complete your mentoring plan. See *How to Harness the Power of Mentoring: A Planner and Journal for Mentees* (available with this book or from my website https://businessmentoringsolution.com).

Based on your inventory of your strengths and limitations, break down the journey into stages. Think of these stages as building blocks to achieve your goal. Remember, this is about working ON, not IN, your business.

What new knowledge and skills do you need for your business? Make a list; for example, basic bookkeeping, marketing on social media, how to do sales, tracking inventory, setting up an Etsy shop. What is most important to do right now? Prioritize the items on your list from most to least critical.

Assess your strengths and assets too. This is just as important as identifying your weaknesses and gaps, perhaps even more so.

Make a list of learning activities that will help you develop your knowledge and skills for each item on the list. Guiding questions are provided on the next page.

Specify a date by which you will complete this task. For example, you may need to take a basic book keeping course so that you can keep track of your revenues and expenses. You can find online home study courses (free) that you can complete within four weeks if you put in six to eight hours per week.

You may also discover that some organizations or government programs offer free training online. The planner/journal for this book will help you keep organized.

MAKE A LIST!

My Strengths

1. Attention to detail but with a clear vision of my future.
2. Good listener and people skills.
3. Skilled at this service.

Where I Need Improvement

1. Bookkeeping and financial tracking.
2. Marketing and promotion, especially digital.
3. Working with suppliers.

My Learning Plan (for each improvement area)

1. What do I need to learn?
2. Outcomes—How I will know I'm successful?
3. How will I learn? (online, classroom, reading, etc.)
4. Schedule for completion?

Harness the Power of Mentoring   65

If you prefer a classroom setting, your local community college or university may have an extension program where you can learn in a classroom. Your chamber of commerce or business development center is another possible source, and some private enterprises may offer small group training.[24]

You decide what is the better option for you, even if it means you need to pay tuition.

What opportunities can help you move forward? Think outside the box. If you need to network—and who doesn't—you may need to join the local chamber of commerce and start going to their business mixers. Pay the membership fee and add the mixer dates to your agenda. Keep track of which ones you go to and how many you miss, as well as new people you meet. Don't lose their business cards!

A friend keeps a book where he writes down the names of people he meets at these mixers and records something memorable about them so that he can follow up. You can use a (free online) CRM (Customer Relations Management) application such as Highrise for this purpose.[25]

YOUR BUSINESS CONCEPT: FIRST STEPS TO A BUSINESS PLAN

A business concept is an idea that addresses an unsolved problem, gap, opportunity, or issue sometimes called "the pain point"[26] but more usually referred to as your **unique value proposition** or **elevator pitch.**

The following three questions will guide you to create your business concept:

1. What is the problem that needs to be solved?

2. What solution do you offer that benefits or gives value to your customer?

3. What are the unique features about your solution that make you stand out from your competitors?

You should be able to describe your business concept briefly and persuasively in 20 to 30 seconds using this formula. It's referred to as an elevator pitch because it was conceived as something you can deliver in a short elevator ride.

> [The pain point is] a yet-to-be-solved burning problem that nothing on the market currently addresses or addresses poorly.
>
> —John Vyge, *The Dragon's Den Guide to Assessing Your Business Concept*, 2012, p.5.

Examine your business concept carefully and compare it to the success factors gleaned from the experiences of hopeful entrepreneurs who made pitches in the Dragons' Den™ TV series as described by John Vyge.[27]

I've added a few other factors to help you think your way from your business concept to a business plan, based on my experiences conducting business start-up workshops.

1. What's the one problem you will solve? What's the pain point?

2. Clearly identify the benefit to your customers or clients who use your product/service. How will you solve that problem?

3. What is unique about what you propose as a solution to the problem?

4. Build a mock-up and show it to others for their feedback.

5. How will you make sure that you have repeat business and a steady cash flow?

6. Identify your ideal customer or client and learn as much as you can about that market segment.

Harness the Power of Mentoring   67

7. Only include the features that your product or service absolutely needs to brand it, eliminate waste, and get it to market quickly.

8. Who do you need to collaborate with so that you can achieve your goals quickly—for example, enlist the help of a mentor and connect with strategic partners.

9. Trigger a rapid increase in sales by finding products and services that complement what you are offering so that you can go along for the ride.

10. Don't get caught unawares. Plan your operations in advance to manage sudden increases in business.

11. Develop a sustainable money-making system as an owner-operator or by licensing your product or service.

12. Finally, write it down! You are more likely to think it through more thoroughly and follow through with your plan if you have a written copy.

NOW WRITE YOUR BUSINESS PLAN

Business experts agree that you need to write a business plan to fledge out your business concept. A business plan challenges you to demonstrate that your business concept is feasible and viable. A business plan describes what you do, who you do it for, how you do it, and the financials (money in, money out).

Find an online template, gather your information, and start to write it. The *Business Model Canvas*[28] is a good place to start. It's a helpful, free, visual aid. You can modify and grow your plan from there if you need more details, for example, to apply for a bank loan.

I like the Business Model Canvas because it's visual, simple, and easily modified. You can play with different scenarios and even mount a copy on your wall!

KEY PARTNERS	KEY ACTIVITIES	VALUE PROVIDED	CUSTOMER RELATIONSHIPS	CUSTOMERS
Who helps you?	What you do	How you help	How you interact	Who you help
	KEY RESOURCES Who you are and what you have		**CHANNELS** How they know you and how you deliver	

COSTS	REVENUE AND BENEFITS
What you give	What you get

The Business Model Canvas

The Business Model Canvas prompts you to consider all the basic parts of a business plan (what you do, for whom, how you do it, and the finances involved) in a visual format. Even if you need a longer, more detailed business plan, it's still a good place to start.

It's easy to use. Just click where indicated in the appropriate square in the online template and a post-it-style notepad will drop down. You can add jot notes, choose a color, edit, whatever you need to do. You can complete this simple exercise in a very short time.

Begin with the **Value Provided** (how you help) square.

This starting point is the unique value proposition you identified earlier in this chapter. Then follow this sequence to complete the template:

Harness the Power of Mentoring   69

- **Customers:**

  Who you help.

- **Channels:**

  How they know/find you and how you deliver.

- **Customer Relationships:**

  How you interact.

- **Revenue and Benefits:**

  What you get.

- **Key Resources:**

  Who you are and what you have.

- **Key Partners:**

  Who helps you.

- **Key Activities:**

  What you need to do.

- **Costs:**

  What you give at what price.

70   Harness the Power of Mentoring

Now stand back and look at the whole picture. Can you see how each element of the Business Model Canvas is connected to the others?

Whatever you want and need to accomplish will be unique to you and so will the path to get there. Your business plan is a perfect topic to discuss with your mentor.

Once you have the key elements in place, you can start to write a narrative business plan and flesh out the financials.

STRUCTURE YOUR MENTORING RELATIONSHIP

To get the most out of your mentoring relationship, bring structure to it. Although these decisions should be collaborative, the mentee should take charge of organizing and directing the meetings.

- Decide, with your mentor, on a clear S.M.A.R.T. goal (Specific, Measurable, Achievable, Realistic/Relevant, and Timely).

- Decide on a reasonable timeline to complete that goal. Will you need six months? A year?

- Decide how often you will meet, for how long (e.g., once per month for two hours for a year), and where. Is a noisy coffee shop going to work for you? Perhaps the local public library has a quiet space you can use.

- Decide on a format for your meetings and develop an agenda. The planner/journal has a template for this purpose.

- Save some time to review each meeting before you adjourn. What worked? What didn't? Why or why not?

- Set a topic or goal for the next meeting.

- At the half-way mark in your mentorship (e.g., at the six-month point if you agreed on a yearlong mentorship), stop and reflect on the following questions:

  o   Should you stay the course or pivot?

Harness the Power of Mentoring   71

- o What do you need to accomplish over the rest of the mentorship?
- o How will you do that?
- Plan for the end of your mentorship and start winding it down at the next to last meeting. Do you want to continue, or have you taken the relationship to its logical end point?

We often need different mentors at different stages of our development. Sometimes, it's time to move on.

WRITE IT DOWN AND SHARE IT

We all need an accountability partner from time to time— someone to say, "So, have you finished that part of your project?" That's another role for your mentor.

As mentioned earlier, studies show clearly that we tend to do the things we write down and share with others.

- Write out your plan and discuss it with your mentor.
- Share your plan with others in your network.
- Use the accompanying planner/journal to keep on track with your plan.

HOW WILL YOU KNOW IF YOU ARE SUCCESSFUL?

Discuss with your mentor how you will benchmark your successes.

- How will you know that you are where you need to be?
- How will you determine you achieved what you needed to do?
- Decide on specific, measurable outcomes and add the dates by which you will be done.
- Reward yourself when you reach a milestone!

In chapter 8 we'll look at evaluating your progress and outcomes in more detail. Use the planner/journal to record your assessments at the right times in your mentorship.

DON'T BE AFRAID TO PIVOT

It's important to remember that a business plan is really a work of fiction. It hasn't happened yet—it's a plan! Don't get so bound to your plan that you are blinded to emerging facts and situations.

Don't be afraid to change directions—pivot—if the facts tell you that would be wise. Most entrepreneurs find that they need to pivot to take advantage of new opportunities or because the facts indicate that what they'd hoped would transpire did not.

As Peter Thomson (the UK's most prolific information product creator) says, you need to figure out if you've grabbed the thick end of a thin wedge or the thin edge of a thick wedge, and act accordingly.

THE RIGHT MENTOR FOR A SOLOPRENEUR IS...

Someone who understands the importance of personal development and business planning from the point of view of a solopreneur's goals.

They help you structure your thinking about both the mentorship and your business concept so that you can develop S.M.A.R.T. goals and chart your progress.

Chapter 6: KEY INSIGHTS

1. Revisit your personal and professional inventory. Make a list of what knowledge, skills, or experience you need. Discuss with your mentor how to best fill these gaps and make a plan that includes dates for completion of each step.

2. Structure your mentoring relationship by deciding on an overall S.M.A.R.T. goal with the support of your mentor.

3. How often will you meet with your mentor? For how long? Where?

4. Develop an agenda for each meeting to keep it on track. At the end of each meeting, talk with your mentor about how the meeting went, what decisions were made, and recap what you need to accomplish before the next meeting.

5. If you've agreed to meet for 12 months, stop and reflect on your progress at the six-month mark. Is your goal still relevant? Are you on track? Do you need to stay the course or pivot?

6. Write out your plan and keep track of your progress using the templates in the planner/journal. Share your goals and the milestones you are working towards with your mentor and others—they will help keep you accountable.

7. At your next to last meeting, start preparing for the closing of the mentoring relationship. Tidy up any unfinished business.

8. In your last meeting, take time to review your learning journey, celebrate your successes, thank your mentor, and plan for the next step in your career as a solopreneur.

If the plan doesn't work,

change the plan,

not the goal.

VIGNETTE – Tony's story

At first, I resisted making a written plan for my mentorship, but my mentor insisted. I'm very glad that I listened to him.

For one thing, having a written plan meant that I didn't have to carry everything around in my head. For another, I could see concrete evidence of my progress.

I also started to keep a journal about my startup. I've never kept a written journal before, but now I understand why it's so powerful. I was able to record my thoughts and questions and the gist of my meetings with my mentor. It made it easier for me to follow up and held me accountable.

There it all was, in black and white.

A goal without a plan is just a wish.

—Antoine de Saint-Exupery, writer, poet, and aviator.

7

Taking and Giving Feedback

Even when it's hard to hear or say

> We all need people who will give us feedback. That's how we improve.
>
> **—Bill Gates**, American business magnate, philanthropist, and principal founder of Microsoft corporation.

Feedback—others' reaction to your actions or behavior—can be given under many different circumstances. Sometimes it's to draw attention to a behavior that causes discomfort; at other times, it's to correct a skill; at other times, feedback acknowledges your progress and encourages you to keep on doing something well.

Feedback can come from your clients or customers about their satisfaction with your service or products as well as from your mentors. Helpful information or criticism can be used to adjust or improve what you are doing so that you continue to make progress towards your goals.

78   Harness the Power of Mentoring

Susan E. DeFranzo said that feedback is important because it is *always* there. You can't avoid it.[29] But you need to be open to feedback, so you can hear what is being said.

You can learn how to give feedback in a positive way, even if you are delivering less than good news, by paying attention to how others give and receive feedback and the reaction the feedback elicits.

As Douglas Stone and Sheila Heen noted in their best-selling book *Thanks for the Feedback: The Science and Art of Receiving Feedback Well*, most feedback feels less like a gift and more like a colonoscopy.[30] In other words, being on the receiving end of feedback can be profoundly challenging. It can be hard to take if it's not positive.

Similarly, over-the-top praise often doesn't ring true and makes us suspicious of the true motives of the person providing feedback to us.

Giving feedback isn't any easier.

However, if delivered in the right tone, at the right time, and in the right context, feedback can be motivating and spur you to improve and reach greater heights.

Given in a flippant, insensitive, and brusque manner, feedback can create awkwardness and defensiveness.

No one likes to feel judged.

AN ESSENTIAL SKILL

Whatever the source and whatever the reason, feedback is an essential part of a healthy and productive mentoring relationship.

Learning how to give and receive feedback, whether it's formal or informal, verbal, written, or the message you give/get from body language, is an essential skill. We swim in a world of feedback at home, online, at work, and at play. You can't get away from performance reviews, comments, glances, and other ways that we give and get feedback every day.

Harness the Power of Mentoring   79

Yet, most of us overthink the feedback we get or try to ignore it. At times, we don't realize how the feedback we are giving to others is being interpreted and are surprised when the recipient reacts with hostility, confusion, or even anger. And, as a solopreneur who works in relative isolation, you may not be accustomed to giving and receiving feedback. You may feel a bit brittle when someone points out a fault or an error.

The good news is you can develop the skills to give and receive feedback in ways that will help you grow and thrive. You can do this IF you master the skills to accept and learn from the feedback given to you. You can learn to disagree in an open and nonconfrontational way. You can learn to give feedback in such a way that others will learn from you.

Approached in the right way, feedback can be the foundation for genuine dialogue and bonding with your mentor. It can present an opportunity for both mentee and mentor to develop new perspectives and insights. The key is to be open, curious, and able to dialogue about feedback, whether it rings true or not.

You don't have to agree with feedback that is given to you, however, nor should you expect feedback that you give to others to be accepted just 'because.' The difference lies in how you approach such a conversation. Avoiding it is not a good solution.

In their book *Crucial Conversations: Tools for Talking When Stakes are High*,[31] Kerry Patterson and his coauthors addressed situations where opposing opinions, strong emotions, and high stakes are present. These factors can sabotage a relationship or cause people to agree to a less-than-optimal solution to which they don't really buy in.[32] This scenario can occur when feedback is given and received!

How do you avoid that trap? How can feedback help you develop a genuine dialogue, and prevent it from paralyzing or destroying a relationship? How can you learn to have crucial conversations that will help you develop an honest, healthy, and productive relationship with your mentor?

FEEDBACK IN A MENTORING RELATIONSHIP

Australian mentoring expert Ann Rolfe described what she has observed over the years about the *mentoring mindset*: a set of attitudes, values, or philosophy with which people approach their roles in a mentoring relationship.

The mentoring mindset values courage, being constructive, accepting differences and responsibility, and working toward developing constructive dialogue.[33]

Can you see how developing a mentoring mindset will help you give and receive feedback? Let's examine the elements of a mentoring mindset more closely:

Courage: Stepping up to a situation even though you are uncomfortable.

Constructive criticism: Building up, not putting down.

Acceptance of Differences: Differences of opinion are healthy. No one else walks in your shoes nor do you walk in those of others.

Acceptance of Responsibility: Hold yourself accountable for your thoughts, words, and deeds.

What's that got to do with feedback? Everything. You will need a clear mentoring mindset to accept and process what others tell you about how they perceive your actions and behaviors.

LEARN HOW TO SOAR

We often think of feedback as focused on our weaknesses, gaps, and failures. But that's a glass half empty approach. It ignores the gifts that you carry and that will help you reach your goals.

Based on the research of Jacqueline Stavros and others, Ann Rolfe reminds us to focus on positives, potential, and opportunity in mentoring, using the acronym SOAR that

SOAR

Strengths

Opportunities

Aspirations

Results

was coined by Stavros and her colleagues.

SOAR refocuses our attention away from gaps, weaknesses, and failures and reminds us to notice positive attributes.

This new direction grew out of *positive psychology*, a therapeutic approach developed by Martin Seligman around twenty years ago that refocused attention from pathology to strength.[34] It's now being applied in many areas of human development, including addictions treatment, and is often termed *a strength-based approach*.

The implications for giving and receiving feedback in a mentoring relationship are enormous. You are not being asked to ignore weaknesses, failures, and gaps. Simply acknowledge that they are part of an overall conversation that includes opportunities and results.

Weaknesses, limitations, and gaps can change if you are willing to put in the effort.

HOW TO GIVE AND TAKE FEEDBACK

Douglas Stone and Sheila Heen made a startling discovery when they set about studying feedback: it's all about the person receiving the feedback. What! It's not about the giver? Not really.

Think about how you feel when you get feedback, particularly those moments just before, when you know it is coming. Feeling unsettled? You bet.

Adrenalin kicks in and the fight or flight response is triggered. Our reactions prevent us from receiving feedback well and engaging in constructive dialogue.

82   Harness the Power of Mentoring

Here's what Stone and Heen learned from their research:

Receiving feedback well is a process of sorting and filtering—of learning how the other person sees things; of trying on ideas that at first may seem a poor fit; of experimenting. And of shelving or discarding the parts of the feedback that in the end seem off or not what you need right now.

Stone and Heen examined how feedback—and how we receive it—is affected by our relationship with the giver, whether we perceive it as true, and whether the feedback concurs with what we believe about ourselves (or not).

In their book *Thanks for the Feedback* (listed in the Appendix as a key resource), Stone and Heen reviewed these triggers in detail and suggest key strategies for handling them more productively.

If handling feedback well is a challenge for you, I suggest you make good use of this particular resource.

HOW TO RESPOND IF YOU DISAGREE

And if you disagree with feedback that is presented to you? Human relations and communication expert Dale Carnegie offered the following advice:[36]

- First, *think before you speak.* Organize your thoughts. What do I think about this? Why? What's the evidence to support my opinion?

- Second, *acknowledge the other person's opinion in a friendly way without agreeing or disagreeing or shutting down conversation.* Avoid using "but," "however," "nevertheless," for example. It's helpful to use reflective listening: "I hear you say that…" Not only does this give you time to organize your thoughts further, but it also slows you down and may help clear up any miscommunication.

- Finally, *when you offer a contrary opinion, provide your evidence immediately without aggression* or in a way that may diminish the other person or, on the other hand, without being passive and giving up your right to your point of view: "From the evidence I've seen..."

Carnegie famously observed that the only way to get the best of an argument is to avoid it. Never say, "You're wrong." Instead, show respect for the other person's opinion.

If you are wrong, admit it and move on.

If you put aside your own ego, you can win others to your point of view.

SAFETY IN A MENTORING RELATIONSHIP

Experts in human relationships agree that individuals must feel safe—physically, mentally, emotionally, and spiritually—for healthy relationships and constructive dialogue to evolve.

Patterson and the coauthors of *Crucial Conversations* observed that it's rarely the message that provokes defensiveness and fear. It's more often the *condition* of the conversation, that is, whether you feel safe hearing the message.

People who are good at dialogue have a gift for noticing whether others feel safe or not and are able to take steps to build a sense of security and trust.

As Patterson and his coauthors noted, "When you don't feel safe, even well-intentioned comments are suspect."[37]

This is one of the paradoxical aspects of getting feedback. Sometimes we feel...grateful, eager, energized. At other times we... [are] hurt, defensive, resentful. Our responses don't always hinge on the skill of the giver or even on what is being said. Rather, they're based on how we are hearing what's said and which kind of feedback we think we are getting.

—David Stone & Sheila Heen, *Thanks for the Feedback: The science and art of receiving feedback well.* 2014, p.30.

THE RIGHT MENTOR FOR A SOLOPRENEUR IS...

Someone who focuses on your positive potential while also acknowledging what you need to do to grow and thrive as an individual who prefers to work alone.

They don't expect you to always agree with them and will listen to your counter-argument respectively.

They work with you to actively create an environment where you feel safe in expressing your opinions and thoughts.

CHAPTER 7: KEY INSIGHTS

1. We receive and give feedback all the time; it can't be avoided. Learning how to give and receive feedback is an essential skill to help you grow and reach your goals.
2. Feedback is the foundation for constructive dialogue with your mentor.
3. Cultivate a mentoring mindset—courageous, constructive, and accepting of differences and responsibilities—so that you are open to feedback, can filter and sort feedback, and respond to feedback in a productive manner.
4. Feedback should SOAR! Focus on strengths, opportunities, aspirations, and results.
5. How we receive feedback is strongly influenced by our relationship with the giver, whether we perceive that the feedback is true, and whether it concurs with our sense of ourselves.
6. Feedback can make us feel defensive or even fearful, particularly if we don't feel safe.
7. If you disagree with feedback, think before you speak. Remember to be respectful and friendly and speak from a point of view that is based on evidence.
8. If handling feedback well is a challenge for you, check out some of the resources cited in this chapter.

VIGNETTE – Ann's story

In our first meeting, our mentors listened to us pitch our idea for a business selling artisan soaps and candles but reacted with silence. We realized in that awful quiet space they were struggling to find the words to tell us that we were all over the map. And we were.

Finally, one of the mentors spoke up. "Have you thought," she asked carefully, "about the potential market for these products and who might be your competitors?" Well, we hadn't. We were so in love with the idea that we'd put our energies into dreams instead of research.

The mentors were very gentle with us in that first meeting. We hadn't had time to develop a relationship with them and barely knew them, so I'm glad they didn't blow us out of the water right away.

As our mentoring relationship grew and deepened and we learned to trust, feel safe, and develop constructive dialogue with our mentors, we were able to have more difficult discussions without becoming defensive. Because we were open to feedback, we were also open to new ideas and opportunities.

Because we felt safe, we trusted our mentors and thought carefully about their feedback. Eventually, we turned our energies to more pragmatic ideas from which we could grow a viable business.

8

Evaluate Your Progress

Learn from mistakes, celebrate successes

> The most serious mistakes are not being made because of wrong answers. The truly dangerous thing is asking the wrong question.
>
> **—Peter Drucker**, one of the best-known and most influential thinkers and writers on management theory and practice.

Formal mentoring programs that operate out of larger workplaces such as multinational corporations usually have a structured evaluation component. Not so the solopreneur who seeks a mentor from a network of business acquaintances.

So, what is a solopreneur to do? Just forget about evaluation?

90   Harness the Power of Mentoring

- Why evaluate?
- What to evaluate?
- When?

WHY EVALUATE?

Evaluation is a process by which you identify and learn from your mistakes and successes. Evaluation helps us to systematically examine whether we've reached our goals: Have we been successful in achieving what we wanted and needed to do in our mentorship?

You can see that for evaluation to be useful, you must have clear goals. You also need to have appropriate criteria to judge your relative success—the right questions. As a solopreneur, you will need to consider your attitude, mindset, and objectives, which differ from those of conventional entrepreneurs. You also need to decide what kind of evaluation you are doing:

- *Outcome evaluation* is about what you achieved in comparison with what you wanted to achieve. Did you achieve the goal you set? Why or why not?

- *Process evaluation*, on the other hand, is about how you got there. This type of evaluation is about the journey, not the destination. What happened along the way? Did you encounter any speed bumps or changes in schedule? Did you need to refocus or pivot?

I suggest you need to do both kinds of evaluation: the outcomes achieved (or not) and how you got there (process). For example, rather than wait until the mentorship is coming to a close, take a few minutes at the end of each meeting with your mentor to review how well that session worked for you.

Did you cover your agenda items? If not, are you equally satisfied that the material or topics you did cover were worth the time?

Do you feel that you moved the goal posts, even a tiny bit?

Through process evaluation, you can learn what enabled you to achieve your goals or, conversely, what did not work well and set you off track.

For example, did you spend most of your time with your mentor complaining or criticizing rather than focusing on constructive dialogue about your mentoring plan?

Did you spend excessive amounts of time on personal issues?

If so, are you surprised that you didn't achieve as much as you had hoped?

On the other hand, if you were committed, well prepared for your meetings, listened carefully, engaged in constructive dialogue, and focused on the goals you agreed upon at the beginning, you should not be surprised that you met or exceeded your objectives for that meeting.

WHEN AND HOW TO EVALUATE A MENTORSHIP

Evaluation of your mentorship works much the same as any other learning experience. For example, consider this list of outcomes-oriented questions to discuss with your mentor during your final meeting:[38]

- Your reaction to the mentorship: Was it a useful experience? Enjoyable?

- What you learned: Did you improve your knowledge and skills?

- Can you put what you learned into action? That is, has your behavior changed?

- Has the mentorship resulted in better business practices and outcomes?

92   Harness the Power of Mentoring

You shouldn't wait until your mentorship is completed before evaluating how it is going, however. Experienced mentors such as David Kay and Roger Hinds[38] suggest that you periodically review the mentoring process and relationship by asking these questions:

- Are you meeting the objectives you set at the beginning of the mentorship?

- Does the timetable seem realistic for both mentee and mentor?

- Has anything happened that caused you to change your original plan?

- What about the boundaries that you agreed upon at the start of the mentorship? Are you able to stay within them?

- Are both you and your mentor OK with how the mentorship is unfolding?

I recommend that you make a habit of asking these questions at the end of each meeting with your mentor. See the planner/journal for a template to help you do this.

If your regular evaluation indicates something is amiss, you can talk with your mentor about how to address the problem. In some situations, you may decide the mentorship isn't working for you. You may choose to bring it to a close early.

Don't stick with a mentorship for the sake of appearances or because you are uncomfortable terminating it.

This is where a mentoring agreement like the one provided in the planner/journal will help. If you have agreed at the start to the circumstances that indicate when the mentoring relationship should end, it will be easier to manage this potentially difficult discussion.

Evaluation is not just about demonstrating success; it is also about learning why things don't work. As such, identifying and learning from mistakes is one of the key parts of evaluation.

Evaluation is not about finding out about everything, but about finding the things that matter.

—State Government of Victoria, Dept. of Sustainability & Environment, Australia (2010).

THE RIGHT MENTOR FOR A SOLOPRENEUR IS...

Someone who will honestly and openly participate in ongoing evaluation of the mentorship and is prepared to act to correct or end the mentorship if it isn't working out.

Chapter 8: KEY INSIGHTS

1. Evaluation is an essential part of a mentorship and helps you learn from your mistakes and successes.

2. Be clear from the outset what you want and need to achieve in the mentorship but be prepared to change your goals if that seems to be the right thing to do.

3. Review and assess every meeting with your mentor so that you are aware of how you are progressing. You may need to tweak your process.

4. At your final meeting with your mentor, discuss—honestly and openly—how you feel about the experience, what you learned, how it has changed your behaviors, and the impact on your business.

5. Don't be afraid to end the mentorship if it is not working to you or your mentor's satisfaction.

VIGNETTE – Phil's story

Something just wasn't right. I couldn't put my finger on it, but I felt I wasn't getting what I needed from the mentorship. But I was too uncomfortable to bring it up with my mentor. He'd put a lot of effort into the mentoring relationship. I needed to do a really honest appraisal of my part in it.

I realized that I wasn't as prepared as I should have been for our meetings. I made excuses…too many demands from my family and new business. I was feeling tired and overwhelmed, so much so that I tended to focus on that rather than on the mentorship goals and what I needed to do to reach them.

I decided to have an honest and open conversation with my mentor—one of those 'difficult conversations' that I usually avoid. He made it easy for me. He agreed on my assessment and said that he'd been waiting for me to bring it up. We decided to recommit to the mentoring relationship and hold ourselves to the tasks I needed to accomplish rather than on talking so much about how I was feeling. He promised me that I would not feel so overwhelmed once I started to see results.

He was right. And we also started to evaluate each meeting to keep on track and on top of things. I'm seeing better results and gaining confidence as a result. And do you know something? I'm not feeling so overwhelmed and have developed some effective strategies for dealing with too many demands on my time.

9

How to Say Thanks and Goodbye

When your mentorship has run its course

> We must find time to stop and thank the people who make a difference in our life.
>
> **—John F. Kennedy**, 35th US President.

The day will come—all too soon—when your formal relationship with your mentor is complete. That day is usually at the end of the agreed-upon schedule (usually 12 months), but it could occur earlier if you feel you've reached your goals or if the mentorship simply isn't working out.

Sometimes you and your mentor may decide to continue the mentoring relationship, formally or informally.

In any of these scenarios, expressing gratitude and appreciation for the time your mentor has given you is plain good manners.

If you are like most of us, you may feel awkward saying thanks to your mentor, let alone writing a card or note to express your gratitude. Just a simple "thank you" will mean a lot to your mentor but consider how much more sincere it would sound if you mention some specifics.

Here are some examples:

"I cannot thank you enough for the time you took to meet with me each month."

"I really appreciated how well you listened and encouraged me to express myself."

"I'm so grateful for what I've learned during this mentorship about how to prioritize and plan."

"Thank you for your guidance, encouragement, and support. I feel much more confident now."

WHEN YOUR MENTORSHIP IS COMING TO THE AGREED-UPON END POINT

Twelve months have passed. You've been meeting regularly each month with your mentor, you've come to each meeting prepared, you've done the work, and you feel you've reached your goals. Your mentor agrees. It's time to wrap up.

You may feel ready to move on. Perhaps you now have the confidence to fly on your own, or you may feel that you need to look for a new mentor who can help you get to the next level.

You may wish to continue with the same mentor.

Whatever the situation, take the time to express your appreciation for what this mentor has helped you achieve. Then have a frank and honest discussion about your next steps.

If you are uncomfortable or uncertain, reach out to a dispassionate third party: a trusted friend or colleague or the mentoring program manager.

Here are some suggestions about how to start the conversation:

1. Going solo

"Because of the work we've done together over the past year, I feel confident to step out on my own."

2. Finding a new mentor

"I've really appreciated your support in helping me get started on my business. Now I feel that I need to focus on marketing and promotion. Can you suggest anyone who has that expertise and might be interested in mentoring me?"

3. Continue the existing mentorship

"Your support and encouragement have meant a lot to me. I'd like to continue to meet with you, if you are interested and have the time."

WHEN YOUR MENTORSHIP CLOSES EARLY

Your mentorship may close earlier than expected for a variety of reasons. Examine your situation carefully. It's important to identify what is going on so you can decide on the best course of action.

• You may have reached your goals more quickly than expected.

If you have reached your goals more quickly than anticipated, you may decide to close the mentorship. Be sure your mentor feels the same. You may be suffering from overconfidence or not realize how much deeper you need to go.

It may be better to focus on a new set of goals for the time remaining.

• You may have discovered that your business idea wasn't feasible.

Sometimes a business idea sounds good but isn't feasible given the market and other conditions at the time. Most ideas don't actually work out in their original form, but if you are intent upon becoming a solopreneur, don't give up (see chapter 1).

Instead of closing the mentorship, consider exploring other ideas with your mentor during the time remaining in your mentorship. Take advantage of your mentor's role as a sounding board.

• Another opportunity may have come up.

Occasionally while you are exploring one idea, an unexpected opportunity comes up.

One mentee with whom I worked had focused on developing a market garden but realized she needed to develop hands-on experience and expertise to make it work.

She was offered an opportunity to work in operations for an established greenhouse business; she jumped at the chance, while making her intentions of eventually starting her own greenhouse business clear to the proprietors (See Jennifer's story, chapter 1). Her employers were very happy to mentor her in learning how to run a greenhouse business.

She now intends to work for the greenhouse for 1-1/2 to 2 years and reassess her readiness to open her own business at that time. She arrived at this decision in discussion with her mentor.

• You may have learned that you aren't ready at this point in your life to become a solopreneur.

Not everyone is cut out to be a solopreneur and that's OK. Better to figure that out early before you spend energy and possibly money trying to be something that you aren't cut out to be!

Harness the Power of Mentoring   101

And at times life just gets in the way: personal relationships, care responsibilities, financial situations, health...all these factors may signal to you that it's not a good choice at this time, or even ever.

Recall the advice that Carol Roth gave in chapter 5: We need to ask ourselves *if we should be an entrepreneur, now or ever.*[40]

If you plan to fly on your own as a solopreneur, ask yourself the same question and be brutally honest in your answer.

• You may feel the relationship with this mentor simply isn't working for you.

Not every mentoring relationship works out the way we hoped. Some of the signs to watch for include:

• Leaving your meetings feeling frustrated or stuck or directionless.

• Dissatisfaction with your progress.

• Feeling anxious and uncomfortable in your meetings.

• Not feeling a connection with your mentor.

If this is what is happening to you, don't waste any more time. Have a frank—yes, and difficult—conversation with your mentor. As the authors of *Crucial Conversations*[41] counsel, start with your heart. Others are rarely the sole source of conflict; by focusing on yourself in the relationship you are more apt to succeed in changing the situation.

This is true simply because *you* are the only entity that *you* can change.

How do you feel about this relationship? What do you really want and need from it? What would it take to refocus, so you get those results? If you were to identify the problems and seek a solution, what would that look like?

102   Harness the Power of Mentoring

One of the hard questions to ask is this: *Is it possible with this mentor?*

Sometimes we aren't compatible with others because of personality or other issues; sometimes we can start anew with that individual. Only you and your mentor can decide what is best and workable at this point.

By the way, closing a mentoring relationship early because of incompatibility between a mentor and mentee isn't a sign of failure. It's simply one of life's lessons.

Effective Communication Skills Checklist ©

- Adopt a friendly tone.

- Let your mentor do most of the talking.

- Show respect for their opinion by expressing interest in their point of view.

- Empathize with their ideas and desires.

- Don't argue!

- Use reflective listening (paraphrasing) to mirror what they are saying and ensure that you understand what they are trying to tell you.

TAKE THE WORRY OUT OF A DIFFICULT CONVERSATION

As solopreneurs, we tend to worry a lot, especially when we don't have someone to bounce solutions off. The thought of having difficult conversations can make us lose sleep at night.

If you are the kind of person who worries excessively about difficult and crucial conversations, ask yourself these questions suggested by Dale Carnegie in his popular book *How to Stop Worrying and Start Living*[42]:

1. What is the worst thing that can possibly happen?

For example, your mentor could feel that they let you down, be really embarrassed or surprised, or feel other strong emotions. They may wish to sever all ties with you, which means you will have lost a potential ally and access to their business network. Further, anticipation of their reaction may cause you to avoid social or business situations where you know they will be present.

2. Prepare yourself to face the worst.

How could you handle the worst-case scenario of a strong negative reaction? Here's what to do: Review the effective communication skills checklist. Practice, practice, practice. If you've put effort into building a good working relationship, trust that it can sustain differences of opinion.

As the authors of the bestseller *Getting to Yes* suggested, if you pay attention to people issues—how you are treating the other person—you can avoid eliciting defensive or reactive behaviors.[43] Treat the other person with respect and empathy for their feelings and focus on the substantive issues that need to be brought out into the open.

3. Try to improve on the worst-case scenario.

What could you do to lighten the tension? Try starting with praise and honest appreciation. Don't blame. Talk about your own mistakes. Use the pronoun "I" rather than "you." Ask questions. Listen well. Try to see what is in the best interests of both parties, mentor and mentee.

And, as Dale Carnegie famously said, "Remind yourself of the exorbitant price you can pay for worry in terms of your health."[44] Finding a way to handle worry about crucial and difficult conversations is a critical skill to develop, particularly for a solopreneur.

It's literally a matter of life and death.

CLOSING YOUR MENTORSHIP

Whatever the reason your mentorship is coming to a close, take the time to do a thorough and honest review with your mentor.

Consider the following questions:

- What did you achieve?
- What was the most important work you did together?
- What was the most important lesson you learned?
- What future challenges do you anticipate?
- How will you apply that learning to resolve future challenges?
- What is the next step to take?

CELEBRATE!

Richard Branson, philanthropist, entrepreneur, and the founder of Virgin, says never underestimate the power of celebrating! Life is better when we stop to appreciate our achievements and milestones.[45]

Harness the Power of Mentoring   105

Good research provides evidence about the positive impact that celebration has on our lives. Celebration reminds us about what is going right. It reminds us of our skills, talents, and abilities. It motivates us to keep on going.

According to psychologist Fred Bryant, as quoted in *Psychology Today*, celebration also builds resilience and helps us to manage daily setbacks and challenges. It helps us to feel optimistic in the face of adversity.[46]

What could be more appropriate than to celebrate the journey you and your mentor completed? In your first meeting together (at least for this mentorship), you laid out some serious goals to accomplish. You likely accomplished many other things along the way, whether it's something relatively intangible such as weathering your first business mixer or something more concrete such completing your business plan or getting your first sale or client.

Awesome.

Mark the occasion and make it a habit to do so as often as possible in the future. Notice your accomplishments and those of others. Be mindful whether the achievement or occasion is big or small.

Think of some special way to pause and say, "Well done!"

THE RIGHT MENTOR FOR A SOLOPRENEUR IS...

Someone with whom you can develop a reciprocal and collaborative working relationship where mentor and mentee appreciate one another's efforts.

Chapter 9: KEY INSIGHTS

1. Expressing gratitude and appreciation is not just good manners; it's a habit you should carry over into your business relationships. It's an acknowledgement that your mentor has devoted time and energy to helping you succeed.

2. When you express thanks, be specific. Refer to the actions and benefits you are grateful to have received.

3. Whether you feel ready to move on upon the completion of your mentorship or feel you still need a mentor (and not necessarily the same one), think through your decision carefully and discuss this with your current mentor. This is an important decision. Decide in haste, repent at leisure!

4. If the mentorship isn't working out, you've discovered that your business idea wasn't feasible, another opportunity has come up, you've reached your goals earlier than anticipated, or you've realized you aren't ready to become a solopreneur (now or ever), you have choices. You can decide to close the mentorship, find a new mentor, or continue working with your current mentor on new objectives.

5. Remember that deciding to close a mentorship earlier than anticipated because of incompatibility is not a sign of failure. But consider discussing your situation with your mentor and, if possible, a dispassionate third party.

6. If you are worried about having a potentially difficult conversation, follow the effective communication skills checklist and think through what you need to say and how best to say it. Practice.

108   Harness the Power of Mentoring

7. As Dale Carnegie advises, remind yourself of the worst that could happen. Then prepare yourself to face that possibility and take steps to improve on the worst-case scenario. Don't pay a price with your health by worrying and not acting when you should.

8. Review with your mentor what you achieved, the most important work you did together, lessons learned, what the future holds, and how you will meet that future.

9. Celebrate! You've earned it!

10. Mark your achievements (and those of others) in a special, memorable way. Make a regular habit of being mindful of big and small occasions to celebrate.

VIGNETTE – Maureen's story

I wasn't happy. I felt anxious before meeting with my mentor and frustrated afterwards. I didn't feel this mentoring thing was working out very well for me.

I knew this situation wasn't doing either me or my mentor any good. I remembered the advice I was given about having difficult conversations and sat down to write out what I thought was the problem:

1. The mentorship wasn't what I expected. I thought it would be more hands-on, you know, like doing things such as writing a business plan together. Instead, my mentor wanted to talk about big picture strategy.

2. When I bring up an issue, I don't always get the kind of response I expect. Instead of saying, "Most small businesses fail because the owner doesn't know how to control the finances," I'd like some concrete advice about options to avoid that kind of failure happening, perhaps seminars or workshops or short courses to take. I don't feel that my mentor understands how scared I am!

I decided that I needed to have one of 'those' conversations with my mentor. It was difficult, but he agreed that he felt the same!

We discovered the root cause of our mutual frustration and anxiety lay in differences in expectations and miscommunication.

We resolved to start again by clarifying our expectations and learning how to listen better and explain needs better.

We also agreed to have this type of conversation more often, regularly, so that we don't fall into the same trap again.

So far, so good.

> It is important at the beginning of any mentoring relationship to agree on the boundaries, the objectives, and the exit strategy...By all means become friendly... but always remember that you need to remain independent and don't become too familiar, otherwise you may start to confuse the issues.
>
> **—David Kay & Roger Hinds**, co-authors of *A Practical Guide to Mentoring: Using Coaching and Mentoring Skills to Help Others Achieve Their Goals.* (5th ed., 2012, p. 108)

10

Next Steps

Am I ready to be a mentor to a solopreneur?

> We make a living by what we get, but we make a life by what we give.
>
> **—Sir Winston Churchill**, British Prime Minister (1940–45, 1951–55), army officer, artist, and writer.

Mentoring relationships may continue for years, although the nature of the relationship changes during that time just as the people involved will grow and change.

You aren't the same person you were two or three years ago, and neither is your mentor. You will have grown in confidence, knowledge, and skills. Your circumstances and interests, and perhaps the focus of your business, may have shifted dramatically.

You may find your relationship with your mentor is no longer a mentoring relationship. It may feel like a peer-to-peer collegial relationship based on your history together and the trust and friendship you built.

Inevitably, the day will come when you think you may be ready to be a mentor yourself. You'd like to give back.

How will you know when it's right to take this next step?

AM I READY TO BE 'THAT' MENTOR?

'That' mentor is someone who understands their role clearly: someone who knows that the best mentors are good listeners and interested in the whole person.

Despite our best intentions, not everyone is cut out to be a mentor. If you intend to take on this challenge, you will want to be the best mentor you can possibly be. You want to be *that mentor* who helps make a real positive difference in the life of a solopreneur.

- First, do you have an honest and sincere desire to help others as you have been helped?

- Second, do you understand the difference between being directive—telling others what to do—versus encouraging others to grow and develop? Are you a good listener?

- Third, do you have the time and energy required? Can you make yourself available on a regular schedule for an extended period, usually up to a year?

If your answer to any of these questions is 'perhaps' or 'maybe' or even 'no,' then being a mentor *at this time* likely isn't a good idea. That's not to say that being a mentor will never be in your stars, just not right now.

That's OK.

Make a note to come back to the idea regularly to make an honest assessment.

PRINCIPLES FOR EFFECTIVE MENTORING

In his book *The Heart of Mentoring*[47], author David A. Stoddard declared that to be effective, mentoring must deal with the whole person and work to develop an individual from the inside out. Too often, mentoring (particularly for business) focuses only on developing a repertoire of behaviors and skills.

Stoddard presented ten principles for developing people to their fullest potential. I've paraphrased the principles here and added a brief note to each one:

1. Living is about giving.
There is no room for self-centeredness in a mentoring relationship. Mentoring is about giving the gift of yourself.

2. Mentoring is a process that requires perseverance.
It really *is* about the journey you are on together. Don't expect a quick fix and be prepared to make mistakes. Learn from them.

3. Mentors open their world to their mentoring partners.
'Come down from the mountain' and share openly, sincerely, and without arrogance. Learn humility.

4. Help mentees find their passion.
Life is too short to spend it doing something that doesn't fulfill you.

5. Help mentees deal with their pain.
Stress, tension, anxiety, and worry can literally end your life. Share experiences and offer comfort and compassion to others who are suffering.

6. Model how to put your personal values into practice in your personal and professional life.
Values, says Stoddard, act as filters and, when used to guide your decisions and actions, will provide the balance needed for you to feel happy and fulfilled.

7. Mentors also model character.
No matter how you define 'character'—and I recommend you think long and hard about what that is—do you walk the talk? Do you encourage your mentee to develop and strengthen character?

8. Mentors affirm the value of spirituality.
A holistic perspective includes the dimension of spirituality in a person's life. One can be spiritual without adhering to any single religious dogma. It's a matter of seeing yourself as part of something bigger, however you define spirituality.

9. Mentors leave a legacy.
They strive to make a positive difference in the lives of others. They also hope their mentees will become mentors someday (the domino effect).

10. Mentors just do it.
No secret formula exists for mentoring effectively. No template will work for everyone, mentor or mentee. Mentoring needs practice and it takes time to develop your own stride, your own way of mentoring.

As you think about whether this is the right time to become a mentor to another solopreneur—or if it will ever be the right time— remember you will continue to grow and learn in that role, and you will also continue to hone your business skills as a solopreneur.

No one expects you to be perfect.

If you worked diligently at your mentorship, followed the steps outlined in this book, and have a passion for what you do, you will likely be THAT mentor who can make a significant and positive difference in another person's life.

THE RIGHT MENTOR FOR A SOLOPRENEUR IS...

Someone who has a desire to give back, leave a legacy, and who understands what drives the solopreneur.

The right mentor is someone who helps the mentee develop from the inside out.

The right mentor for a solopreneur could be YOU!

Chapter 10: KEY INSIGHTS

1. Mentoring relationships evolve as the mentoring partners grow and change. Don't be surprised if you realize one day that your mentor is your mentor no longer.

2. Think long and hard about whether becoming a mentor is a good idea for you. Is the timing right for you? Do you have a sincere and burning desire to make a positive impact in another's life?

3. Solopreneurs have a lot on their plate, but also much to give back to others like them. If you decide this is not the right time, don't let the prospect slip off your radar screen. Revisit the idea from time to time.

4. Consider what qualities the most effective mentors possess. Do you also? If not or partially, would being a mentor help you develop these qualities, perhaps to a higher level?

5. Principles-based mentoring is more effective than a simple list of mentoring qualities or skills. The reason is that principles encourage us to work with the whole person to help them develop from the inside out. This approach also helps you to develop and grow as a mentor.

VIGNETTE – Carol Ann's story

My relationship with my mentor was easy. We continue to meet once every two months for a coffee; our mentoring relationship has evolved into a professional friendship. We are more peers than mentor and mentee now.

One day, my (former) mentor asked me if I had ever considered being a mentor myself. I really hadn't thought about it. As a solopreneur, I'm a Jill-of-all-trades and there aren't enough hours in the day as it is. It's all I can do to squeeze in the occasional coffee date!

But the more I think about it, the more becoming a mentor appeals to me. Being a solopreneur can be lonely and isolating. This would force me to get out at least once a month.

More than that, however, I realize that I really want to 'pay it forward.' I've benefited so much from the support of my mentor. I believe that the experience of a mentoring relationship was a critical factor in my becoming a successful business person and the more mature and confident person that I am today. Is it time to pay back?

I'd really like to make the kind of positive impact on another person's life that my mentor made on mine. Something to think about.

To the Reader:

Did you enjoy reading this book?

Did you learn something new from it?

Did it cause you to rethink what you already know and do?

Please email your comments/review to me at: author@thebusinessmentoringsolution.com

I value your feedback!

In return for your review, I will send you a complimentary copy of my eBook *Harness the Power of Mentoring: Top TIPS for Solopreneurs*.

Supporting Solopreneur Success

Afterword

We've come a long way from the old mentor/protégé model of mentoring! The new model of developmental mentoring pioneered by visionaries such as David Clutterbuck, David Megginson, Bob Garvey, Ann Rolfe, Lois Zachary, and David A. Stoddard presents us with an alternate approach. Developmental mentoring is more in line with contemporary ideas about what solopreneurs want to achieve and how we can best get there.

It's more about values and vision, empowerment, holistic personal and professional growth, character building, individual agency, self-determination, relationships, and paying it forward.

The focus of this book is on what you need to know to find and work with the right mentor for you. This means developing a healthy, productive relationship with someone who understands the mindset, attitude, objectives, and business practices of a solopreneur.

Other books in this series expand on this theme. The second is for your mentor: *Be That Mentor! How to Mentor the Solopreneur (Without Losing Your Mind)*. The third is for someone who manages a business mentoring program at the community level. That person might work for a chamber of commerce or other organization that supports entrepreneurs: *The Art of Managing a Mentoring Program for Solopreneurs: A Guide for the Community-Based Mentoring Program Manager*.

Although these resources are meant for others in your mentoring network, you may find they will help you, the solopreneur, understand and work more effectively within these relationships because you have better insight into their roles.

The fourth book addresses a critical issue for anyone involved in a mentoring relationship in the 21st century: diversity of gender, culture, ethnicity, age, ability, sexuality, and so on (*Barrier-Free Business Mentoring for Everyone*). In writing this final book in the series, I drew on my 45 years of learning and working as a practicing applied anthropologist and the experience and expertise of others.

These subsequent books in this series will be available in 2019 and 2020 in either print or digital (downloadable) form from my website. Audiobooks will be available too. Please watch for them!

A planner/journal and 'Tips' booklet accompanies each book in the series to help you stay on track and reach your goals. You'll find a list of further resources at the end of each book.

Publication of these and other resources to help you on your mentoring journey will be announced in my free monthly newsletter. Sign up on my webpage: https://businessmentoringsolution.com.

Thank you for investing your trust, time, energy, and money to allow me to share what I've learned and practiced as a solopreneur, mentee, mentor, and mentoring program manager.

I welcome your feedback and would enjoy hearing about your mentoring experiences.

Virginia (Ginny) McGowan PhD
Charlottetown
Prince Edward Island
Canada

Appendix

Resources to Support Your Mentorship

This Appendix is structured to help you access a wide variety of resources that will help you, the solopreneur, work with your mentor in a healthy mentoring relationship.

Because it's my preferred mentoring model, I've chosen books and other information products that support developmental mentoring. It's not an exhaustive list but will help you begin exploring the world of mentoring. Other mentoring resources may be offered by your local chamber of commerce or business association, so check for locally-available resources too. Don't forget the endnotes in this book that provide information on the resources mentioned in the text.

I highly recommend reading widely outside of the business mentoring domain. Books such as Dan Pontefract's *Open to Think: Slow Down, Think Creatively, and Make Better Decisions* (2018, eBook published in Vancouver BC by Bright Wing Books) is a wonderful resource for mentor and mentee.

I've annotated this list to help you decide if a resource is what you are looking for.

I've also rated each resource but remember that this rating is only my opinion.

- Business Mentoring Programs

- Business Mentoring

- Learning Styles

- Solopreneur-Focused Blogs

- Business Planning

- Business Planning Templates

BUSINESS MENTORING PROGRAMS

International Mentoring Association

http://mentoringassociation.org

The IMA Is a nonprofit association of mentoring professionals in education, business, and government now housed at the University of Florida in the USA.

Members can access monthly webinars, curated research, personalized suggestions, annual conferences with member discounts, and networking opportunities. The IMA offers two publications: *Connect* and *The Link*.

A range of membership levels are offered including individual and student memberships. Two levels of accreditation for mentoring programs and certification for consultants and trainers are available for a fee.

Cherie Blair Foundation for Women: Mentoring Women in Business Programme

http://www.cherieblairfoundation.org/programmes/mentoring/

The Cherie Blair Foundation for Women is an organization dedicated to empowering women entrepreneurs in developing and emerging economies. They've reached more than 140,000 women to date across more than 100 countries.

One of their signature programs is Mentoring Women in Business. Mentors are screened and receive online training (and must pass a quiz upon completion of the training) before being matched with a mentee for a one-year mentorship. For example, although based in Canada, I was matched with a woman solopreneur in Kenya during my first year as a mentor with this program with whom I met once monthly for an hour online via Skype or Google Hangout.

No charge for participation. Volunteer participants have the benefit of an exceptional platform that offers profiles of mentors and mentees, a Q&A Forum, a library of key resources on mentoring and business topics, and webinars (e.g., "Understanding Business Growth Models").

Women Mentor Association

http://womenmentorassociation.org/index.html

WMA is a nonprofit charitable organization that offers a mentorship program for women and girls facing social and professional barriers. Their program is designed to support female entrepreneurs in business globally develop skills, access funding, build confidence, and network. It's a volunteer-based organization with a small team of employees, and offers opportunities for mentors or mentees, volunteer involvement in long- or short-term projects, and 'ambassadors'.

WMA offers short-term internships in science, engineering, and technology; training and workshops for members on a range of topics; mentoring; and international outreach. Their 2018 campaigns include African Women and Girls in STEM and Mental Wellness.

As a relatively new organization, WMA is still developing some of its online features, but recent blogs are worth checking out.

Forum for Women Entrepreneurs

http://www.fwe.ca

The Forum for Women Entrepreneurs (FWE) is a Vancouver-based charity that educates, mentors, and connects women entrepreneurs to be wildly successful, promoting strong economies and thriving communities.

The Programs and Events at FWE are designed to support and mentor women who are venturing into new business opportunities or ready to ramp up and grow their existing business. From start-up advice to specific tips and tricks, FWE leaders, advisors, and business professionals are ready to share their expertise.

Founded in 2002, FWE has been educating, mentoring, and empowering women entrepreneurs for over 15 years. With 400+ E-Series Program participants, 1,600+ pairings through the FWE Mentor Program, FWE supports over 1,500+ women each year.

In January 2016, FWE became a registered charity (861056646RR0001).

FWE offers a mentoring program nationally across Canada with volunteer mentors and a fee-for-service for mentees. For details, see http://www.fwe.ca/programs/mentor-program/

Young Agrarians

www.youngagrarians.org

[From the website] Young Agrarians (YA) is a Canadian grassroots initiative made up of farmers, food activists, community organizers, food lovers, and balcony and community gardeners. YA aggregates data for the ecological farm sector across Canada, posts opportunities and content on our farmer blog, and works to engage an inspiring network of new and young farmers, food growers, homesteaders, and farm lovers.

In BC, YA offers a business mentorship program that pairs up new farms in start-up with experienced mentors.

MicroMentor

https://www.micromentor.org

Launched in 2009, MicroMentor is an online free nonprofit social network that connects entrepreneurs and volunteer business mentors in more than 190 countries across the globe. MM claims to have more than 30,000 connections, created thousands of jobs, and generated millions in revenue.

The organization is supported by corporate, government, and nonprofit partners.

Futurpreneur Canada

https://www.futurpreneur.ca

Note: I reached out to Futurpreneur Canada after participating in their Mentoring Masterclass. This is what they had to say about what they offer:

We get it: learning to be an entrepreneur is not always easy. That's why from business plan to business success, Futurpreneur offers what young entrepreneurs need to get their start-up off the ground.

We are a national, non-profit organization that provides financing, mentoring and support tools to aspiring business owners aged 18–39, and our internationally recognized mentoring program matches young entrepreneurs with a business mentor from a network of more than 3000 volunteer mentors.

Futurpreneur entrepreneurs receive up to two full years of business mentoring support as they gain access to the financing they need to launch and grow their businesses. Our experienced mentors help entrepreneurs build confidence, overcome difficult challenges and strengthen business acumen.

Our array of online mentoring resources is designed to support crucial conversations for mentoring pairs at different stages in their relationships. Resources such as our

Mentoring Canvas, crafted with the input from mentors across Canada helps pairs create a plan for their mentoring journey; mentoring case studies; mentoring guides for mentors and entrepreneurs and many other tools are all there to support the mentoring process for aspiring entrepreneurs' learning journey into entrepreneurship.

The Lonely Entrepreneur

https://lonelyentrepreneur.com

The Lonely Entrepreneur describes itself as a learning community. In addition to live weekly video coaching sessions, they offer 150 training modules, tools and templates, vendor and software reviews, and a 24-hour online community.

Michael Dermer is the founder and offers one-on-one coaching among other services.

An annual subscription fee applies.

SCORE

https://www.score.org

SCORE, a resource partner of the U.S. Small Business Administration, is a nonprofit organization comprising a network of volunteer and expert business mentors that has helped more than ten million entrepreneurs since 1964. Currently, SCORE has over 300 chapters across the U.S.

Their online matching service either pairs you with the right mentor or allows you to search for a mentor. Volunteer mentors can sign up on the website.

As well as in-person events in their chapters, SCORE offers live and recorded webinars and online courses in their Business Learning Center library.

128   Harness the Power of Mentoring

BOOKS ON BUSINESS MENTORING

Blanchard, K., & Diaz-Ortiz, C. (2017). *One Minute Mentoring: How to Find and Work with a Mentor—and Why You'll Benefit from Being One.* US: William Morrow.

ISBN 978-0-00-814681-8.

160 pages.

Also available in hardcover, eBook (Kindle), and audiobook formats.

As with Ken Blanchard's bestseller *The One Minute Manager*, this book presents a fictional parable. This time, it's a tale of a mentee's relationship with his mentor in an intergenerational workplace mentoring situation.

It's a quick and easy read, and you can find a used copy for a good price. Good advice for career mentoring.

Clutterbuck, D. (2014). *Everyone Needs a Mentor (5th ed.).* London, UK: Chartered Institute of Personnel and Development.

ISBN 978-1-843983-66-8

201 pages.

Also available as an eBook (Kindle).

From one of the world's leading expert on developmental mentoring, this best-selling book, originally published in 1985, is now in its fifth edition. Although this book addresses some of the community aspects of mentoring, including starting up a business, its primary target is workplace-based mentoring programs.

Harness the Power of Mentoring   129

Clutterbuck's definition of mentoring, his discussions of the different models and many benefits of mentoring, is useful for anyone thinking about entering a mentoring relationship. For example, he discusses the expectations that are brought to the mentorship by both parties, mentor and mentee, about the purpose of the mentorship, their roles and behaviors, and likely outcomes, all within the context of a developmental relationship.

Various sections of interest to solopreneurs discuss what makes an effective mentor and mentee, how to begin, when and what to review (evaluate), phases of the mentoring relationship, problems often encountered, diversity issues, e-mentoring, and what happens after the mentorship comes to an end.

The text includes case studies as an Appendix and a comprehensive bibliography and index.

Highly recommended resource from an established subject matter expert and clear writer.

Clutterbuck, D. (2013). *Making the Most of Developmental Mentoring: A Practical Guide for Mentors and Mentees*. Liverpool, UK: Wordscapes.

ISBN 978-0-9576945-0-7

72 pages.

Only available as an eBook (Kindle).

In this helpful little book Professor Clutterbuck clarifies many of the key concepts of mentoring: what do we mean by 'mentoring'? What is developmental mentoring? What is the difference between mentoring and coaching? What is the role of reflection in mentoring? What are the benefits of mentoring?

Recommended for anyone new to mentoring or developmental mentoring or who are interested in the history of mentoring. Readers will enjoy Professor Clutterbuck's straightforward and practical presentation. As with most mentoring resources, the emphasis is on workplace-based mentoring, but the key lessons about developmental mentoring are transferable to mentoring for the solopreneur.

Garvey, B., Stokes, P., & Megginson, D. (2009). *Coaching and Mentoring: Theory and Practice.* Thousand Oaks, CA: Sage.

ISBN 978-1-4129-1216-7.

272 pages.

For those who want to know more about the research and scholarly literature on coaching and mentoring from the perspective of a British research team, this book is the definitive authority. Each chapter highlights a different method and includes case studies and thorough analyses.

The book is divided into four sections: an introduction that addresses the main differences between coaching and mentoring, a review of organizational and practice issues, contemporary debates, and emerging issues. In keeping with the action-oriented approach of the British/European mentoring community, this book is heavily influenced by the authors' own experiences. Some themes explored are the role of power in the paired relationship, transference and counter-transference tendencies, conversational learning, goal setting, and diversity.

Highly recommended for practitioners, particularly those who conduct research on mentoring or design mentoring programs.

Zachary, L.J., & Fischler, L.A. (2009). *The Mentee's Guide: Making Mentoring Work for You*. San Francisco, CA: Jossey-Bass.

ISBN 978-0-34358-6.

148 pages.

Also available as an eBook (Kindle).

In this third book in Lois Zachary's trilogy (the previous two were for mentors and organizations, respectively), the author and her colleague Lory Fischler provide an in-depth review of the benefits of mentoring related to work and professional development.

As with most other mentoring guides, this book is largely directed towards workplace-based mentoring. Nonetheless, it is an insightful guide to making the most of your mentoring relationship. It's intended to help mentees take a more active role and includes stories and exercises. Highly recommended.

LEARNING STYLES

Zachary, L. with L.A. Fischler. (2009). *The Mentee's Guide: Making Mentoring Work for You*. San Francisco, CA: Jossey-Bass.

ISBN 978-0-34358-6.

148 pages.

Also available as an eBook (Kindle).

Although designed with a workplace-based mentoring program in mind, chapter two (Preparing Yourself to Make the Most of Mentoring) will work for the solopreneur also, especially the section on learning styles (pp. 32–37).

A SAMPLE OF SOLOPRENEUR-FOCUSED BLOGS

One Woman Shop (with Cristina and Sara)

Sound advice for the female solopreneur. Highly recommended starting place for any gender identity!
https://onewomanshop.com/

Think Creative Collective (with Abagail and Emylee)

Help for creative entrepreneurs to build a profitable business by organizing chaos. Resources, posts, courses, podcasts, and webinars. http://thinkcreativecollective.com/dashboard

Tara Gentile

Weekly advice and support for small business owners (CoCommercial), podcast (What Works), and What Works Business Immersion (an inquiry-based approach to learning about your business). http://taragentile.com/

Meera Kothand

Simplified marketing strategies for bloggers and solopreneurs with digital products and services. Thousands of subscribers to her swipe file of handpicked email content ideas.
https://www.meerakothand.com/

Femtrepreneur (with Mariah Coz)

Guide to digital product ideas (online courses and more).
https://www.femtrepreneur.co/

byRegina (with Regina Anaejionu)

Solid advice on branding, copy, and content strategies for an online business. http://byregina.com/

Making Sense of Cents (with Michelle Schroeder-Gardner)

Financial and legal advice. Monthly blog with more than 300,000 followers. https://www.makingsenseofcents.com

A SAMPLE OF BUSINESS PLANNING BOOKS

Wilson, L. (2011). *The Small Business Planner:The Complete Entrepreneurial Guide to Starting and Operating a Successful Small Business.* New York, NY: Morgan James Publishing.

ISBN 978-1-60037-905-5.

202 pages.

Also available as an eBook.

Larry Wilson, a successful entrepreneur, wrote a practical and comprehensive guide to starting a small business. As one of the reviewers noted, he breaks starting a small business down into digestible pieces. The writing is clear, concise, and reflects the author's background as a mentor, consultant, columnist, and college business instructor.

For example, the book includes helpful check lists for starting a small business complete with dos and don'ts, a list of the most common marketing mistakes, and numerous templates. Short and to the point, this book is recommended for those who are new to the small business world

Tryge, J. (2012). *The Dragons' Den Guide to Assessing Your Business Concept*. Mississauga, ON: John Wiley & Sons Canada Ltd.

ISBN 978-1-118298-80-0

Also available as an eBook.

324 pages including index.

The producers of the hit CBC TV show Dragons' Den™ compiled case studies and use a workshop-style approach to illustrate ten key factors for successful small business planning. They discerned these factors from their experiences with 'pitchers' to the Den—entrepreneurs who asked the Dragons for financial support for their product or service.

If you are looking for a step-by-step guide to understanding successful business planning, this book is for you. Clear and concise, loaded with tips and advice, the case studies are well-chosen and informative. The first section helps you develop a sound business concept. The rest of the book includes sections on conducting a feasibility study, developing a product roadmap, defining your market, and developing a market strategy. Self-study workshops are included in each chapter to help you work out the lessons.

The concluding chapter recaps the ten success factors and prompts you to summarize your business concept according to the success factors. An extensive glossary is very helpful, as are the endnotes that point to either the sources of information cited or suggestions for where to go for more on a particular subject.

If you wish to plan your business in more detail, the authors point you to their companion guide: *The Dragons' Den Guide to Investor-Ready Business Plans*.

Genadinik, A. (2018). *How to Write a Business Plan: Business Planning Made Simple*. Author.

ISBN: 1-51-974178-2/978-1-51-974178-3.

150 pages.

Also available as an eBook (Kindle).

From a top designer of business planning apps and online courses is a very simple guide to creating a business plan. His focus is on helping you organize your ideas—always good to do! Alex also points out the benefits of having a mentor to help you through this process.

Written in clear and simple language, this book strips down a business planning process to its key ingredients, based on the author's own entrepreneurial experiences. Chapter 9 ("Making you a better entrepreneur & starting your business") is particularly helpful for first-time startups as he pokes the reader to think about business risks, your ego, stress and failure, and surrounding yourself with the right people among other topics.

The appendices include a list of additional resources and a full business plan example for a mobile app company. One of the chapters is structured as a business plan that you can use to write your own. Recommended for startups.

By the way, this book is now used by the University of Kentucky entrepreneurship program.

A SAMPLE OF BUSINESS PLANNING TEMPLATES/ GUIDES

The Economist (downloadable pdf):

http://library.uniteddiversity.coop/Business_Plans/Guide_to_ Business_Planning.pdf

Entrepreneur e-magazine:

https://www.entrepreneur.com/article/247574

BPlans:

https://www.bplans.com/sample_business_plans.php

YouTube:

https://www.youtube.com/watch?v=PDWvcsTloJo

https://www.youtube.com/watch?v=pTKvgsUrLGE

U.S. Small Business Administration:

https://www.sba.gov/tools/business-plan/1

SCORE:

https://www.score.org/resource/business-plan-template-startup-business

Inc.:

https://www.inc.com/larry-kim/top-10-business-plan-templates-you-can-download-free.html

Harness the Power of Mentoring   137

Canvanizer (My all-time favorite free template source):

https://canvanizer.com/

U.S. Small Business Administration:

https://www.sba.gov/about-sba

Bplans:

https://www.bplans.com/downloads/business-plan-template/

The Balance:

https://www.thebalancesmb.com/entrepreneur-simple-business-plan-template-4126711

My Own Business Institute:

https://www.scu.edu/mobi/business-plans/

SCORE:

http://100startup.com/resources/business-plan.pdf

Plan Builder:

https://planbuildr.com/business-plan/new

PandaDoc:

https://www.pandadoc.com/business-plan-templates/

138   Harness the Power of Mentoring

InvoiceBerry:

https://www.invoiceberry.com/free-business-plan-templates

Scotiabank:

http://getgrowingforbusiness.scotiabank.com/business-planning/

CIBC:

https://www.cibc.com/en/small-business/advice-centre/
business-planning-guide.html

Canada Business Network (Government of Canada):

https://canadabusiness.ca/business-planning/sample-business-
plans-and-templates/

Small Business BC:

https://smallbusinessbc.ca/article/how-write-a-business-plan/

LawDepot:

https://www.lawdepot.ca/contracts/business-plan/

Innovation, Science, and Economic Development Canada:

https://www.canada.ca/en/services/business/start/planning.html

Business in a Box:

https://www.biztree.com/pricing/

Products and Services

The Business Mentoring Solution is committed to helping solopreneurs realize their true potential. What I shared with you in this book comes from the heart, from a passion for helping others succeed.

This is just one of several ways that I help. Please contact me for other services offered, such as:

- Training (workshops and seminars).

- Online courses about mentoring.

- Mentoring program design, implementation, and evaluation

- Speaking engagements for groups / organizations.

- Information products (Books, Planners/Journals, 'Top TIPS' eBooks).

Contact Me!

If you would like additional information about how to apply the insights I shared in this book, learn how to exercise these values, concepts, and approaches in your life and business, or if you would like information on other services and information products offered by *The Business Mentoring Solution*, please contact me at:

Virginia McGowan PhD

The Business Mentoring Solution
255 Richmond Street
Charlottetown Prince Edward Island
Canada C1A 1J7

Phone: +1-902-566-5462
Talk/Text: +1-902-330-2013
Email: author@thebusinessmentoringsolution.com

Website and free monthly Newsletter:
https://businessmentoringsolution.com

Join Me Online

Twitter: @vmcgowanphd to find updates, resources, advice, and snippets for solopreneur and mentoring success!

LinkedIn: https://www.linkedin.com/in/virginiamcgowanphd/

Facebook: https://www.facebook.com/Virginia-M-McGowan-PhD-The-Business-Mentoring-Solution-432161290588196/

Sign up for my **free monthly newsletter** that includes tips on mentoring and news about updates and new information products at:

https://businessmentoringsolution.com

For Orders and Inquiries

✦ **Email:** author@thebusinessmentoringsolution.com

◊ **Text or cellphone:** +1-902-330-2013

☏ **Landline telephone:** +1-902-566-5462

⌂ **Postal:** The Business Mentoring Solution
255 Richmond Street, Charlottetown PE Canada C1A 1J7

Please send the following books/information products.

I understand that I may return any of them for a full refund, for any reason, no questions asked.

_____

_____

Please send more FREE information on:

• Other books or information products

• Speaking engagements

• Workshops and seminars (training)

• Consulting

Harness the Power of Mentoring   143

Next, for your order to be processed, please fill out the contact information on the following page.

*Indicates required field. Please print.

*Your Name:

_____

*Your Mailing Address:

_____

*City or Town:

_____

State/Province:

_____

*Country:

_____

*Zip/Postal Code:

_____

*Email address:

_____

You will be contacted via **email** with further information on placing an order.

Only **PayPal** payments accepted (you don't need to set up a PayPal account to do this).

Sales tax and shipping fees may apply.

Index

advice 16, 22, 25, 47, 53, 82, 101, 109
advisory 35
arrogance 52, 113
benefit 12, 42, 54, 65-66, 68, 69, 107, 117
Blanchard, Ken 46
Branson, Richard 104
Bryant, Fred 105
business mentoring 40, 62, 120
Business Model Canvas 67-68, 70
Business 2 Community 3
Challenges 12, 32, 35, 47, 52, 60, 67, 104, 105
Campbell Hanley, Maureen vi, x
Canfield, Jack 19, 21
Carnegie, Dale 30, 82, 103-104, 108
Champagne, Matt i
Cherie Blair Foundation for Women viii, x, 45, 62
Churchill, Sir Winston iii
Clutterbuck, David 1, x, 8, 18, 41, 53, 120
Couture, Joseph 20, 22
coaching 2, 16, 30, 110
collaborative 14, 41, 53, 57, 70, 106
communication 52, 53, 58, 82, 102-103, 107, 109
competitor 30, 52, 65, 87
confidence 6, 9, 15, 25, 51, 54, 96, 98-99, 111
conflict 30, 101, 140
Crucial Conversations 79, 83, 101, 103
decisions 4, 6-9, 11, 13, 19, 34, 37, 42, 47, 53-54, 70, 74, 113
DeFranzo, Susan E. 78
de Saint-Exupery, Antoine 76
development 3-4, 6-8, 48, 53, 62, 65, 71, 73, 81, 120
    personal development 73
    professional development 4, 7, 53
developmental mentoring 8, 48, 120
Diaz-Ortiz, Claire 46
Dragons' Den 31, 66
Drucker, Peter 89
Effective Communication Skills Checklist 102-103, 107
elevator pitch 65-66
entrepreneur(s) 1-4, 6-7, 9-12, 17, 29, 31, 32, 42, 44, 51-53, 55, 57, 58, 62, 66, 73, 90, 101, 104
entrepreneurial 2, 9, 31, 53
entrepreneurship 12, 17, 58
evaluation 89-95

process evaluation 90-91
    outcome evaluation 90
Evans, Suzanne 30
fail 1, 6, 62, 109
failure(s) 6, 9, 32, 54, 80-81, 102, 107, 109, 135
fear 5-6, 83, 86
fearful 15
fearless 28
feedback 2, 5, ,66, 77-82, 84, 86-87
financial 6, 29, 31, 35, 37, 40, 44, 64, 67, 70, 101
Forum for Women Entrepreneurs viii, 44, 52, 124
Frankl, Victor 20, 22
Garvey, Bob iii, x, 120
Gates, Bill 77
goals 2, 19, 24-25, 52, 55, 58, 61, 63, 67, 73-74, 77
goodbye 2, 97
guide 2, 6, 14, 36, 42, 65, 66, 110, 113
guidelines 3
Heen, Sheila 78, 81-82, 84
Hinds, Roger 92, 110
Home-based business 6
humility 52, 113
insights 6, 12, 26, 38, 42, 48-49, 51, 58, 74, 79, 79, 86, 95, 107, 116
intrapreneur 2, 10, 17
inventory 7, 28-30, 32, 38, 51, 55, 63, 74
Irving, Robert K. 9
Kay, David 92, 110
Kearley, S. Paul iii
Kennedy, John F. 97
Lawrence, Doug ii, x
Layton-Turner, Marci 3
Leinweber, Nancy i, x, xi
listening 18, 22, 53, 82, 102
Mandela, Nelson 9
Megginson, David x, 120
mentee(s) 2, 8, 11, 14, 16-17, 41-42, 45-46, 52, 54, 63, 70
mentor 1-2, 5-16, 23, 25, 28, 31-32, 35-37, 40-52
mentoring 2, 3, 5-6, 8, 14, 16, 36, 41-46, 48-49, 51
mentored 42, 48
mentorship 6-8, 15, 19, 45
mentoring models

146 Harness the Power of Mentoring

one-on-one 62
peer mentoring 62
mentoring relationship 2, 5, 16, 23, 36, 41-42,
  44-45, 51-55, 58, 62, 70, 74, 78, 80-81,
  83, 87, 92, 96-97, 101-102, 110-111, 113,
  116-117, 120
Merrick, Lis iv
milestones 52, 74, 104
mindset 3-4, 7, 11-12, 29, 35, 53, 80, 86, 90
Mission Publishing xi
naysayers 12
needs 2, 5, 7, 28, 43, 52-53, 58-59, 62, 65, 67,
  109, 114
network 3-4, 44, 53-54, 58, 65, 71, 89, 103,
  120
networking 4, 53, 58
Obama, Barack 39
Open Thinking 8, 11, 13
Open to Think 8
operation 1, 15, 67, 100
outcomes 27, 51, 64, 71-72, 90-91, 129
Patterson, Kerry 79, 83
plan
  mentoring plan 61, 63, 91
  business plan 40, 61, 65-68, 70, 72-73,
  105, 109
business concept 31, 40, 65-67, 73
strategy 12, 34-35, 45, 61, 109-110, 134
Pontefract, Don ii, 8, 122
Prince Edward Island Business Women's
Association v, ix, x
problems 15, 21, 32, 34-35, 37, 53, 101
dealing with 34
proprietor 1, 17, 100
protégé 41, 120
purpose(s) 19-29, 65, 70
purpose statement 21, 26
Rampton, John 32
Robbins. Mike 27
Rolfe, Ann 80, 120
Roth, Carol 55, 101
reach 13, 17, 22, 35, 38, 40, 44, 48, 62
  reached 10, 90, 97-99, 107
  reaches 16
  reaching 2, 35
risk(s) 3, 5, 17, 32-34, 38
role model 53
Seligman, Martin 81
Setty, Rajesh 51
S.M.A.R.T. 70, 73-74
SOAR 80-81, 86
solopreneur 1-7, 9, 11-12, 15, 17, 23, 25, 29,
  32, 34-35, 37, 40-41, 43, 47, 49-50, 53-58,

61, 73, 75, 79, 85, 89-90, 94, 100-101, 103,
  106-107, 111-112, 114-117
sole proprietor 17
small business owner 2, 6
Stavros, Jacqueline 80-81
Stoddard, David A. x, 113, 120
Stone, Douglas 78, 81-82, 84
strengths 6, 9-10, 17, 38, 63-64, 81, 86
success(es) 2, 6-7, 9, 12-13, 19, 22-23, 52, 61,
  66, 71, 75, 89-90, 93, 95
succeed 1, 5, 7, 16-17, 30-31, 42, 56, 101, 107
successful 6-7, 10, 31-32, 34-35, 40, 49, 52,
  54, 64, 71, 90, 117
thanks 2, 78, 82, 84, 97-98, 107
thinking 2, 6, 8, 11, 13, 16, 30, 42, 47, 54, 73
  Open to Think 8, 122
  Open Thinking 8, 11, 13
Thomson, Peter 72
transform 6, 43
transformative 6, 43
trust 54-55, 58, 83, 87, 103, 111
trusted 48
trusting 13
trustworthy 11-17, 57
unique value proposition 65, 68
values 1, 9, 19-20, 24-25, 29, 80, 113, 120
vision 9, 19, 21-25, 27, 29, 32, 35, 53, 55-56,
  64, 120
Vyge, John 66
wealth 31-33, 38
work 3-6, 10, 12-13, 17, 19, 26, 28, 30, 32,
  34, 36, 38, 40, 42, 45, 49, 51-52, 55, 58, 60,
  70, 72, 75, 78, 85, 91, 93, 100, 104, 108,
  113-114, 116, 120-121
worked 55, 70, 90, 100, 114
working 3, 10, 13, 28, 30, 35, 51, 54, 56, 63-
  64, 74, 80, 92, 94-95, 97-101, 103, 106-
  107, 109
workplace 3, 89
works 31, 34, 35, 52, 62, 79, 91, 101
work style 32, 34
Whittaker, Phil iv
Zachary, Lois J. x, 14, 16, 41, 59, 120

Endnotes

Chapter One

[2] https://www.startupcan.ca/wp-content/uploads/2012/01/Statistics-on-Small-Business-in-Canada_StartupCanada.pdf

[3] https://www.entrepreneur.com/article/280134

[4] Rampton, J. (May 15, 2015). Four Differences Between a Solopreneur and an Entrepreneur Working Alone. Entrepreneur. https://www.entrepreneur.com/article/245766

[5] Layton-Turner, M. (July 2, 2017). Five Major Differences Between Solopreneurs and Entrepreneurs. Business2Business. https://www.business2community.com/startups/5-major-differences-solopreneurs-entrepreneurs-01870776

[6] Belt, P., Paloniemi, K., & Sinisammal, J. (Sept. 2015). One-Person Enterprises and Business Growth. J. of Enterprising Culture, 23(3): 381. https://doi.org/10.1142/S0218495815500132

[7] Hakabyan, M. (Nov. 6, 2017). Who is a Solopreneur or Entrepreneur? Solopreneur. https://www.solopreneurs.co/who-solopreneur-solo-entrepreneur/

[8] Statistic Brain Research Institute. (24 January 2016). Startup Business Failure Rate by Industry. Statistic Brain, Research Institute, www.statisticbrain.com/startup-failure-by-industry/

[9] Langowitz, N., & Minneli, N. (2007). The Entrepreneurial Propensity of Women. Entrepreneurship, Theory and Practice, 24 April. doi: 10.1111/j.1540-6520.2007.00177.x

[10] Further to the guidance in chapters 2 and 3, the accompanying planner/journal for this book provides exercises to help you with the discernment process.

148   Harness the Power of Mentoring

[11] Pontefract, D. (2018). Open to think: Slow down, think creatively, and make better decisions. Vancouver, BC: Bright Wings Books. (eBook location 148 0r 4595)

[12] Ibid.

[13] Available at https://www.management-mentors.com/resources/coaching-mentoring-differences

Chapter Two

[14] Frankl, V.E. (1946). Man's search for meaning. Vienna, Austria: Verlag für Juden und Volk.

[15] Couture, R., & McGowan V. (2013). A metaphoric mind: Selected writings of Joseph Couture. Edmonton, AB: Athabasca University Press.

[16] Canfield, J. 10 Life Purpose Tips to Help You Find Your Passion. http://jackcanfield.com/blog/finding-life-purpose/

[17] https://suzanneevanscoaching.org/

Chapter Three

[18] Tyges, J. (2012). The Dragons' Den Guide to Assessing Your Business Concept. Mississauga, ON: John Wiley & Sons Canada Ltd.

[19] Rampton, J. 5 Personality Traits of an Entrepreneur. https://www.forbes.com/sites/johnrampton/2014/04/14/5-personality-traits-of-an-entrepreneur/#576426303bf4

Chapter Four

[20] Once the mentorship has run its course, you can always enter into a business relationship with someone who was your mentor. Just don't do it while you are in a mentoring relationship with that person. It's a genuine conflict of

interest on their part. After all, they are supposed to be helping you succeed in your business.

[21] http://www.fwe.ca/

[22] http://www.cherieblairfoundation.org/

[23] Roth, C. (2012). The Entrepreneur Equation: Evaluating the Realities, Risks, and Rewards of Having Your Own Business. Dallas, TX: BenBella Books, Inc.

Chapter Five

[24] For example, local business associations may offer in-class small group business basics training.

[25] CRM is a customer relations management database; an example is Highrise by Basecamp.

Chapter Six

[26] Vyge, J. (2012). The Dragons' Den Guide to Assessing Your Business Concept. Mississauga, ON: John Wiley & Sons Canada, Ltd. p.3.

[27] Ibid. The factors listed in that book are identified in this list with an *.

[28] You can download a free template online at www.canvanizer. com.

Chapter Seven

[29] DeFranzo, S. (February, 2016). The Importance of Feedback. Snap Surveys. https://www.snapsurveys.com/blog/the-importance-of-feedback/#more-10942

[30] Stone, D., & Heen, S. (2014). Thanks for the Feedback: The Science and Art of Receiving Feedback Well. US: Viking Penguin.

150   Harness the Power of Mentoring

[31] Patterson, K., Grenny, J., McMillan, R., Switzler, A. (2012). Crucial Conversations: Tools for Talking When Stakes are High. (2nd ed.). Toronto, ON: McGraw-Hill.

[32] Ibid.

[33] Rolfe, A. (2012). Mentoring Mindset, Skills and Tools. Mentoring Works: Australia. Available from www.mentoring-works.com

[34] Seligman, M.E. (2002). Positive Psychology, Positive Prevention, and Positive Therapy. Handbook of Positive Psychology, 2, 3-12. Available from http://www.positiveculture.org/uploads/7/4/0/7/7407777/seligrman_intro.pdf

[35] Stone, D., & Heen, S. (2014). Thanks for the Feedback: The Science and Art of Receiving Feedback Well. US: Viking Penguin. p.17

[36] Dale Carnegie & Associates, Inc. (2014). Skills for Success: Participant Manual. (p. 5.6). Hauppauge, NY: Dale Carnegie & Associates Inc.

[37] Patterson, K., Grenny, J., McMillan, R., Switzler, A. (2012). Crucial Conversations: Tools for Talking When Stakes are High. (2nd ed.). Toronto: McGraw-Hill. pp. 55-58.

Chapter Eight

[38] Kirkpatrick, D.L. (1959). Techniques for Evaluating Training Programmes. Journal of the American Society of Training Directors, 13:3-26.

[39] Kay, D., & Hinds, R. (2012). A Practical Guide to Mentoring: Using Coaching and Mentoring Skills to Help Others Achieve Their Goals. (5th ed.) Begbroke, Oxford: How to Books Ltd.

Chapter Nine

[40] Roth, C. (2012). The Entrepreneur Equation: Evaluating the Realities, Risks, and Rewards of Having Your Own Business. Dallas, TX: BenBella Books, Inc.

[41] Patterson, K., Grenny, J., McMillan, R., Switzler, A. (2012). Crucial Conversations: Tools for Talking When Stakes are High. (2nd ed.). New York: McGraw-Hill.

[42] Carnegie, D. (1981). Combined Edition: How to Win Friends and Influence People; How to Stop Worrying and Start Living. (Rev. ed.). USA: Dale Carnegie & Associates Ltd.

[43] Fisher, R., Ury, W., Patton, B. (2011). Getting to Yes: Negotiating Agreement Without Giving In. (3rd revised ed.). USA: Penguin Books.

[44] Carnegie, D. (2013). Dale Carnegie's Golden Book. USA: Dale Carnegie & Associates Ltd. p. 5

[45] Branson, R. (December 22, 2016). My top ten quotes on celebrating Virgin. https://www.virgin.com/richard.branson/my-top-10-quotes-celebrating

[46] Campbell, P. (December 2nd, 2015). Why You Should Celebrate Everything. https://www.psychologytoday.com/ca/blog/imperfect-spirituality/201512/why-you-should-celebrate-everything

Chapter Ten

[48] Stoddard, D.A. (2003). The Heart Of Mentoring: Ten Proven Principles For Developing People To Their Fullest Potential. Colorado Springs, CO: NAVPRESS.

CPSIA information can be obtained
at www.ICGtesting.com
Printed in the USA
LVHW051920160419
614417LV00002B/2